# GOD'S ANSWERS
## for Your Life

THOMAS NELSON
*Since 1798*

NASHVILLE   DALLAS   MEXICO CITY   RIO DE JANEIRO   BEIJING

Published in Nashville, Tennessee, by Thomas Nelson. Thomas Nelson is a registered trademark of Thomas Nelson, Inc.

Compiled and edited by Kay Wheeler Kilgore.
Page design by Mandi Cofer.

Thomas Nelson, Inc., titles may be purchased in bulk for educational, business, fund-raising, or sales promotional use. For information, please e-mail SpecialMarkets@ThomasNelson.com.

Scripture quotations are from *The Holy Bible, New King James Version.*

ISBN 978-1-4041-8791-7

*Printed in China*

09 10 11 12 13  RRD  9 8 7 6 5 4 3 2 1

# CONTENTS

# Beginning
# in Christ

# How to Know You Are Born-Again

That if you confess with your mouth the Lord Jesus and believe in your heart that God has raised Him from the dead, you will be saved.

For with the heart one believes unto righteousness, and with the mouth confession is made unto salvation.

For the Scripture says, "Whoever believes on Him will not be put to shame."

*Romans 10:9–11*

Most assuredly, I say to you, he who hears My word and believes in Him who sent Me has everlasting life, and shall not come into judgment, but has passed from death into life.

*John 5:24*

Therefore, if anyone is in Christ, he is a new creation; old things have passed away; behold, all things have become new.

*2 Corinthians 5:17*

For by grace you have been saved through faith, and that not of yourselves; it is the gift of God, not of works, lest anyone should boast.

For we are His workmanship, created in Christ Jesus for good works, which God prepared beforehand that we should walk in them.

*Ephesians 2:8—10*

Whoever believes that Jesus is the Christ is born of God, and everyone who loves Him who begot also loves him who is begotten of Him.

By this we know that we love the children of God, when we love God and keep His commandments.

For this is the love of God, that we keep His commandments. And His commandments are not burdensome.

For whatever is born of God overcomes the world. And this is the victory that has overcome the world—our faith.

Who is he who overcomes the world, but he who believes that Jesus is the Son of God?

This is He who came by water and blood—Jesus Christ; not only by water, but by water and blood. And it is the Spirit who bears witness, because the Spirit is truth.

He who has the Son has life; he who does not have the Son of God does not have life.

*1 John 5:1—6, 12*

Therefore whoever confesses Me before men, him I will also confess before My Father who is in heaven.

And he who does not take his cross and follow after Me is not worthy of Me.

He who finds his life will lose it, and he who loses his life for My sake will find it.

*Matthew 10:32, 38–39*

I have been crucified with Christ; it is no longer I who live, but Christ lives in me; and the life which I now live in the flesh I live by faith in the Son of God, who loved me and gave Himself for me.

*Galatians 2:20*

Having been born again, not of corruptible seed but incorruptible, through the word of God which lives and abides forever.

*1 Peter 1:23*

For you are all sons of God through faith in Christ Jesus.

For as many of you as were baptized into Christ have put on Christ.

There is neither Jew nor Greek, there is neither slave nor free, there is neither male nor female; for you are all one in Christ Jesus.

*Galatians 3:26–28*

And those who are Christ's have crucified the flesh with its passions and desires.

If we live in the Spirit, let us also walk in the Spirit.

*Galatians 5:24–25*

I will give you a new heart and put a new spirit within you; I will take the heart of stone out of your flesh and give you a heart of flesh.

I will put My Spirit within you and cause you to walk in My statutes, and you will keep My judgments and do them.

*Ezekiel 36:26–27*


We know that we have passed from death to life, because we love the brethren. He who does not love his brother abides in death.

*1 John 3:14*


But he who received seed on the good ground is he who hears the word and understands it, who indeed bears fruit and produces: some a hundredfold, some sixty, some thirty.

*Matthew 13:23*


Knowing this, that our old man was crucified with Him, that the body of sin might be done away with, that we should no longer be slaves of sin.

For he who has died has been freed from sin.

Now if we died with Christ, we believe that we shall also live with Him.

*Romans 6:6–8*


And that you put on the new man which was created according to God, in true righteousness and holiness.

*Ephesians 4:24*

Fight the good fight of faith, lay hold on eternal life, to which you were also called and have confessed the good confession in the presence of many witnesses.

*1 Timothy 6:12*

Let us hold fast the confession of our hope without wavering, for He who promised is faithful.

*Hebrews 10:23*

If you know that He is righteous, you know that everyone who practices righteousness is born of Him.

*1 John 2:29*

# How to Know the Sufficiency of Jesus

Looking unto Jesus, the author and finisher of our faith, who for the joy that was set before Him endured the cross, despising the shame, and has sat down at the right hand of the throne of God.

*Hebrews 12:2*

And Jesus said to them, "I am the bread of life. He who comes to Me shall never hunger, and he who believes in Me shall never thirst."

*John 6:35*

Let your conduct be without covetousness; be content with such things as you have. For He Himself has said, "I will never leave you nor forsake you."
So we may boldly say:
"The LORD is my helper;
I will not fear.
What can man do to me?"
Jesus Christ is the same yesterday, today, and forever.

*Hebrews 13:5–6, 8*

Seeing then that we have a great High Priest who has passed through the heavens, Jesus the Son of God, let us hold fast our confession.

For we do not have a High Priest who cannot sympathize with our weaknesses, but was in all points tempted as we are, yet without sin.

Let us therefore come boldly to the throne of grace, that we may obtain mercy and find grace to help in time of need.

*Hebrews 4:14–16*

And He said to me, "My grace is sufficient for you, for My strength is made perfect in weakness." Therefore most gladly I will rather boast in my infirmities, that the power of Christ may rest upon me.

*2 Corinthians 12:9*

And Jesus came and spoke to them, saying, "All authority has been given to Me in heaven and on earth.

Go therefore and make disciples of all the nations, baptizing them in the name of the Father and of the Son and of the Holy Spirit,

teaching them to observe all things that I have commanded you; and lo, I am with you always, even to the end of the age." Amen.

*Matthew 28:18–20*

Do not be afraid; I am the First and the Last.

I am He who lives, and was dead, and behold, I am alive

forevermore. Amen. And I have the keys of Hades and of Death.

*Revelation 1:17–18*

I can do all things through Christ who strengthens me.

*Philippians 4:13*

For in Him dwells all the fullness of the Godhead bodily;
and you are complete in Him, who is the head of all principality and power.

*Colossians 2:9–10*

I am the good shepherd. The good shepherd gives His life for the sheep.

*John 10:11*

The LORD is my shepherd; I shall not want.
He makes me to lie down in green pastures;
He leads me beside the still waters.
He restores my soul;
He leads me in the paths of righteousness
For His name's sake.
Yea, though I walk through the valley of the shadow of death,
I will fear no evil;
For You are with me;
Your rod and Your staff, they comfort me.

*Psalm 23:1–4*

Therefore if the Son makes you free, you shall be free indeed.

*John 8:36*

And we have such trust through Christ toward God.

Not that we are sufficient of ourselves to think of anything as being from ourselves, but our sufficiency is from God.

*2 Corinthians 3:4–5*

But the Lord stood with me and strengthened me, so that the message might be preached fully through me, and that all the Gentiles might hear. Also I was delivered out of the mouth of the lion.

And the Lord will deliver me from every evil work and preserve me for His heavenly kingdom. To Him be glory forever and ever. Amen!

*2 Timothy 4:17–18*

My help comes from the LORD,
Who made heaven and earth.
He will not allow your foot to be moved;
He who keeps you will not slumber.

*Psalm 121:2–3*

Jesus said to him, "I am the way, the truth, and the life. No one comes to the Father except through Me."

*John 14:6*

In Him was life, and the life was the light of men.

*John 1:4*

According to the grace of God which was given to me, as a wise master builder I have laid the foundation, and another builds on it. But let each one take heed how he builds on it.

For no other foundation can anyone lay than that which is laid, which is Jesus Christ.

*1 Corinthians 3:10—11*

The night is far spent, the day is at hand. Therefore let us cast off the works of darkness, and let us put on the armor of light.

Let us walk properly, as in the day, not in revelry and drunkenness, not in lewdness and lust, not in strife and envy.

But put on the Lord Jesus Christ, and make no provision for the flesh, to fulfill its lusts.

*Romans 13:12—14*

The LORD is your keeper;
The LORD is your shade at your right hand.
The LORD shall preserve you from all evil;
He shall preserve your soul.
The LORD shall preserve your going out and your coming in
From this time forth, and even forevermore.

*Psalm 121:5, 7—8*

Therefore My Father loves Me, because I lay down My life that I may take it again.

No one takes it from Me, but I lay it down of Myself. I have power to lay it down, and I have power to take it again. This command I have received from My Father.

*John 10:17—18*

The next day John saw Jesus coming toward him, and said, "Behold! The Lamb of God who takes away the sin of the world!

This is He of whom I said, 'After me comes a Man who is preferred before me, for He was before me.'"

*John 1:29–30*

Whom have I in heaven but You?
And there is none upon earth that I desire besides You.
My flesh and my heart fail;
But God is the strength of my heart and my portion forever.

*Psalm 73:25–26*

For there is one God and one Mediator between God and men, the Man Christ Jesus.

*1 Timothy 2:5*

# How to Know the Power of the Word

For the word of God is living and powerful, and sharper than any two-edged sword, piercing even to the division of soul and spirit, and of joints and marrow, and is a discerner of the thoughts and intents of the heart.

*Hebrews 4:12*

Your word I have hidden in my heart,
That I might not sin against you.
I will delight myself in Your statutes;
I will not forget Your word.

*Psalm 119:11, 16*

How sweet are Your words to my taste,
Sweeter than honey to my mouth!
Through Your precepts I get understanding;
Therefore I hate every false way.
Your word is a lamp to my feet
And a light to my path.

*Psalm 119:103—105*

The words of the LORD are pure words,
Like silver tried in a furnace of earth,

Purified seven times.
You shall keep them, O Lord,
You shall preserve them from this generation forever.

*Psalm 12:6–7*

In the beginning was the Word, and the Word was with God, and the Word was God.

He was in the beginning with God.

All things were made through Him, and without Him nothing was made that was made.

In Him was life, and the life was the light of men.

*John 1:1–4*

And that from childhood you have known the Holy Scriptures, which are able to make you wise for salvation through faith which is in Christ Jesus.

All Scripture is given by inspiration of God, and is profitable for doctrine, for reproof, for correction, for instruction in righteousness,

that the man of God may be complete, thoroughly equipped for every good work.

*2 Timothy 3:15–17*

By the word of the Lord the heavens were made,
And all the host of them by the breath of His mouth.

*Psalm 33:6*

He sent His word and healed them,
And delivered them from their destructions.

Oh, that men would give thanks to the LORD for His goodness,
And for His wonderful works to the children of men!

*Psalm 107:20–21*

Forever, O LORD,
Your word is settled in heaven.
Your faithfulness endures to all generations;
You established the earth, and it abides.

*Psalm 119:89–90*

Your testimonies are wonderful;
Therefore my soul keeps them.
The entrance of Your words gives light;
It gives understanding to the simple.

*Psalm 119:129–130*

As newborn babes, desire the pure milk of the word, that you may grow thereby,
if indeed you have tasted that the Lord is gracious.

*1 Peter 2:2–3*

You are already clean because of the word which I have spoken to you.

*John 15:3*

Having been born again, not of corruptible seed but incorruptible, through the word of God which lives and abides forever,

because
"All flesh is as grass,
And all the glory of man as the flower of the grass.
The grass withers,
And its flower falls away,
But the word of the LORD endures forever."
Now this is the word which by the gospel was preached to you.

*1 Peter 1:23–25*

But He answered and said, "It is written, 'Man shall not live by bread alone, but by every word that proceeds from the mouth of God.'"

*Matthew 4:4*

Heaven and earth will pass away, but My words will by no means pass away.

*Luke 21:33*

It is the Spirit who gives life; the flesh profits nothing. The words that I speak to you are spirit, and they are life.

*John 6:63*

Then Jesus said to those Jews who believed Him, "If you abide in My word, you are My disciples indeed.
And you shall know the truth, and the truth shall make you free."

*John 8:31–32*

By faith we understand that the worlds were framed by the word of God, so that the things which are seen were not made of things which are visible.

*Hebrews 11:3*

The grass withers, the flower fades,
But the word of our God stands forever.

*Isaiah 40:8*

Anxiety in the heart of man causes depression,
But a good word makes it glad.

*Proverbs 12:25*

Sanctify them by Your truth. Your word is truth.

*John 17:17*

Hold fast the pattern of sound words which you have heard from me, in faith and love which are in Christ Jesus.

*2 Timothy 1:13*

So then faith comes by hearing, and hearing by the word of God.

*Romans 10:17*

And do not be conformed to this world, but be transformed by the renewing of your mind, that you may prove what is that good and acceptable and perfect will of God.

*Romans 12:2*

And having shod your feet with the preparation of the gospel of peace;

above all, taking the shield of faith with which you will be able to quench all the fiery darts of the wicked one.

And take the helmet of salvation, and the sword of the Spirit, which is the word of God.

*Ephesians 6:15–17*

# What the Holy Spirit Is to You

But the fruit of the Spirit is love, joy, peace, longsuffering, kindness, goodness, faithfulness,

gentleness, self-control. Against such there is no law.

And those who are Christ's have crucified the flesh with its passions and desires.

If we live in the Spirit, let us also walk in the Spirit.

*Galatians 5:22–25*

But as it is written:

"Eye has not seen, nor ear heard,

Nor have entered into the heart of man

The things which God has prepared for those who love Him."

But God has revealed them to us through His Spirit. For the Spirit searches all things, yes, the deep things of God.

For what man knows the things of a man except the spirit of the man which is in him? Even so no one knows the things of God except the Spirit of God.

Now we have received, not the spirit of the world, but the Spirit who is from God, that we might know the things that have been freely given to us by God.

These things we also speak, not in words which man's

wisdom teaches but which the Holy Spirit teaches, comparing spiritual things with spiritual.

But the natural man does not receive the things of the Spirit of God, for they are foolishness to him; nor can he know them, because they are spiritually discerned.

*1 Corinthians 2:9–14*

If you ask anything in My name, I will do it.

If you love Me, keep My commandments.

And I will pray the Father, and He will give you another Helper, that He may abide with you forever—

the Spirit of truth, whom the world cannot receive, because it neither sees Him nor knows Him; but you know Him, for He dwells with you and will be in you.

I will not leave you orphans; I will come to you.

But the Helper, the Holy Spirit, whom the Father will send in My name, He will teach you all things, and bring to your remembrance all things that I said to you.

*John 14:14–18, 26*

But if the Spirit of Him who raised Jesus from the dead dwells in you, He who raised Christ from the dead will also give life to your mortal bodies through His Spirit who dwells in you.

The Spirit Himself bears witness with our spirit that we are children of God,

and if children, then heirs—heirs of God and joint heirs with Christ, if indeed we suffer with Him, that we may also be glorified together.

For I consider that the sufferings of this present time are not worthy to be compared with the glory which shall be revealed in us.

Likewise the Spirit also helps in our weaknesses. For we do not know what we should pray for as we ought, but the Spirit Himself makes intercession for us with groanings which cannot be uttered.

Now He who searches the hearts knows what the mind of the Spirit is, because He makes intercession for the saints according to the will of God.

*Romans 8:11, 16—18, 26—27*

And it shall come to pass in the last days, says God,
That I will pour out of My Spirit on all flesh;
Your sons and your daughters shall prophesy,
Your young men shall see visions,
Your old men shall dream dreams.
And on My menservants and on My maidservants
I will pour out My Spirit in those days;
And they shall prophesy.

*Acts 2:17—18*

Nevertheless I tell you the truth. It is to your advantage that I go away; for if I do not go away, the Helper will not come to you; but if I depart, I will send Him to you.

And when He has come, He will convict the world of sin, and of righteousness, and of judgment:

of sin, because they do not believe in Me;

of righteousness, because I go to My Father and you see Me no more;

of judgment, because the ruler of this world is judged.

I still have many things to say to you, but you cannot bear them now.

However, when He, the Spirit of truth, has come, He will guide you into all truth; for He will not speak on His own authority, but whatever He hears He will speak; and He will tell you things to come.

He will glorify Me, for He will take of what is Mine and declare it to you.

All things that the Father has are Mine. Therefore I said that He will take of Mine and declare it to you.

A little while, and you will not see Me; and again a little while, and you will see Me, because I go to the Father.

*John 16:7–16*

For our gospel did not come to you in word only, but also in power, and in the Holy Spirit and in much assurance, as you know what kind of men we were among you for your sake.

And you became followers of us and of the Lord, having received the word in much affliction, with joy of the Holy Spirit.

*1 Thessalonians 1:5–6*

For everyone who asks receives, and he who seeks finds, and to him who knocks it will be opened.

If a son asks for bread from any father among you, will he

give him a stone? Or if he asks for a fish, will he give him a serpent instead of a fish?

Or if he asks for an egg, will he offer him a scorpion?

If you then, being evil, know how to give good gifts to your children, how much more will your heavenly Father give the Holy Spirit to those who ask Him!

*Luke 11:10—13*

And being assembled together with them, He commanded them not to depart from Jerusalem, but to wait for the Promise of the Father, "which," He said, "you have heard from Me;

for John truly baptized with water, but you shall be baptized with the Holy Spirit not many days from now."

Therefore, when they had come together, they asked Him, saying, "Lord, will You at this time restore the kingdom to Israel?"

And He said to them, "It is not for you to know times or seasons which the Father has put in His own authority.

But you shall receive power when the Holy Spirit has come upon you; and you shall be witnesses to Me in Jerusalem, and in all Judea and Samaria, and to the end of the earth."

*Acts 1:4—8*

For it is not you who speak, but the Spirit of your Father who speaks in you.

*Matthew 10:20*

So shall they fear
The name of the LORD from the west,
And His glory from the rising of the sun;
When the enemy comes in like a flood,
The Spirit of the LORD will lift up a standard against him.

*Isaiah 59:19*

See that you do not refuse Him who speaks. For if they did not escape who refused Him who spoke on earth, much more shall we not escape if we turn away from Him who speaks from heaven.

*Hebrews 12:25*

Who also made us sufficient as ministers of the new covenant, not of the letter but of the Spirit; for the letter kills, but the Spirit gives life.

Now the Lord is the Spirit; and where the Spirit of the Lord is, there is liberty.

But we all, with unveiled face, beholding as in a mirror the glory of the Lord, are being transformed into the same image from glory to glory, just as by the Spirit of the Lord.

*2 Corinthians 3:6, 17–18*

For the Holy Spirit will teach you in that very hour what you ought to say.

*Luke 12:12*

And when they had prayed, the place where they were assembled together was shaken; and they were all filled with the Holy Spirit, and they spoke the word of God with boldness.

Now the multitude of those who believed were of one heart and one soul; neither did anyone say that any of the things he possessed was his own, but they had all things in common.

And with great power the apostles gave witness to the resurrection of the Lord Jesus. And great grace was upon them all.

*Acts 4:31–33*

Therefore do not be unwise, but understand what the will of the Lord is.

And do not be drunk with wine, in which is dissipation; but be filled with the Spirit,

speaking to one another in psalms and hymns and spiritual songs, singing and making melody in your heart to the Lord,

giving thanks always for all things to God the Father in the name of our Lord Jesus Christ.

*Ephesians 5:17–20*

From whom the whole body, joined and knit together by what every joint supplies, according to the effective working by which every part does its share, causes growth of the body for the edifying of itself in love.

And do not grieve the Holy Spirit of God, by whom you were sealed for the day of redemption.

*Ephesians 4:16, 30*

Knowing this first, that no prophecy of Scripture is of any private interpretation, for prophecy never came by the will of man, but holy men of God spoke as they were moved by the Holy Spirit.

*2 Peter 1:20–21*

But you, beloved, building yourselves up on your most holy faith, praying in the Holy Spirit,

keep yourselves in the love of God, looking for the mercy of our Lord Jesus Christ unto eternal life.

*Jude 20–21*

Behold, I send the Promise of My Father upon you; but tarry in the city of Jerusalem until you are endued with power from on high.

*Luke 24:49*

# How to Abide in Christ

Abide in Me, and I in you. As the branch cannot bear fruit of itself, unless it abides in the vine, neither can you, unless you abide in Me.

I am the vine, you are the branches. He who abides in Me, and I in him, bears much fruit; for without Me you can do nothing.

If anyone does not abide in Me, he is cast out as a branch and is withered; and they gather them and throw them into the fire, and they are burned.

If you abide in Me, and My words abide in you, you will ask what you desire, and it shall be done for you.

*John 15:4—7*

And now, little children, abide in Him, that when He appears, we may have confidence and not be ashamed before Him at His coming.

*1 John 2:28*

I love those who love me,
And those who seek me diligently will find me.

*Proverbs 8:17*

I will meditate on Your precepts,
And contemplate Your ways.
I will delight myself in Your statutes;
I will not forget Your word.

*Psalm 119:15–16*

Let the word of Christ dwell in you richly in all wisdom, teaching and admonishing one another in psalms and hymns and spiritual songs, singing with grace in your hearts to the Lord.

*Colossians 3:16*

But those who wait on the LORD
Shall renew their strength;
They shall mount up with wings like eagles,
They shall run and not be weary,
They shall walk and not faint.

*Isaiah 40:31*

Now by this we know that we know Him, if we keep His commandments.

He who says, "I know Him," and does not keep His commandments, is a liar, and the truth is not in him.

But whoever keeps His word, truly the love of God is perfected in him. By this we know that we are in Him.

He who says he abides in Him ought himself also to walk just as He walked.

*1 John 2:3–6*

Draw near to God and He will draw near to you. Cleanse your hands, you sinners; and purify your hearts, you double-minded.

*James 4:8*

For in Him we live and move and have our being, as also some of your own poets have said, "For we are also His offspring."

*Acts 17:28*

Blessed is the man who listens to me,
Watching daily at my gates,
Waiting at the posts of my doors.

*Proverbs 8:34*

Till I come, give attention to reading, to exhortation, to doctrine.

*1 Timothy 4:13*

But put on the Lord Jesus Christ, and make no provision for the flesh, to fulfill its lusts.

*Romans 13:14*

As newborn babes, desire the pure milk of the word, that you may grow thereby.

*1 Peter 2:2*

But be doers of the word, and not hearers only, deceiving yourselves.

*James 1:22*

Speaking to one another in psalms and hymns and spiritual songs, singing and making melody in your heart to the Lord,

giving thanks always for all things to God the Father in the name of our Lord Jesus Christ.

*Ephesians 5:19–20*

And you know that He was manifested to take away our sins, and in Him there is no sin.

Whoever abides in Him does not sin. Whoever sins has neither seen Him nor known Him.

*1 John 3:5–6*

Whoever transgresses and does not abide in the doctrine of Christ does not have God. He who abides in the doctrine of Christ has both the Father and the Son.

*2 John 1:9*

For all things are for your sakes, that grace, having spread through the many, may cause thanksgiving to abound to the glory of God.

Therefore we do not lose heart. Even though our outward man is perishing, yet the inward man is being renewed day by day.

*2 Corinthians 4:15–16*

Therefore we must give the more earnest heed to the things we have heard, lest we drift away.

For if the word spoken through angels proved steadfast, and every transgression and disobedience received a just reward,

how shall we escape if we neglect so great a salvation, which at the first began to be spoken by the Lord, and was confirmed to us by those who heard Him.

*Hebrews 2:1–3*

Looking unto Jesus, the author and finisher of our faith, who for the joy that was set before Him endured the cross, despising the shame, and has sat down at the right hand of the throne of God.

*Hebrews 12:2*

# How to Build Your Faith

Now faith is the substance of things hoped for, the evidence of things not seen.

By faith we understand that the worlds were framed by the word of God, so that the things which are seen were not made of things which are visible.

But without faith it is impossible to please Him, for he who comes to God must believe that He is, and that He is a rewarder of those who diligently seek Him.

By faith he forsook Egypt, not fearing the wrath of the king; for he endured as seeing Him who is invisible.

*Hebrews 11:1, 3, 6, 27*

That the genuineness of your faith, being much more precious than gold that perishes, though it is tested by fire, may be found to praise, honor, and glory at the revelation of Jesus Christ,

whom having not seen you love. Though now you do not see Him, yet believing, you rejoice with joy inexpressible and full of glory,

receiving the end of your faith—the salvation of your souls.

*1 Peter 1:7—9*

For in it the righteousness of God is revealed from faith to faith; as it is written, "The just shall live by faith."

*Romans 1:17*

Have I not commanded you? Be strong and of good courage; do not be afraid, nor be dismayed, for the LORD your God is with you wherever you go.

*Joshua 1:9*

So then faith comes by hearing, and hearing by the word of God.

*Romans 10:17*

If any of you lacks wisdom, let him ask of God, who gives to all liberally and without reproach, and it will be given to him.

But let him ask in faith, with no doubting, for he who doubts is like a wave of the sea driven and tossed by the wind.

For let not that man suppose that he will receive anything from the Lord;

he is a double-minded man, unstable in all his ways.

*James 1:5—8*

For with God nothing will be impossible.

*Luke 1:37*

We are hard-pressed on every side, yet not crushed; we are perplexed, but not in despair;

persecuted, but not forsaken; struck down, but not destroyed—

always carrying about in the body the dying of the Lord Jesus, that the life of Jesus also may be manifested in our body.

*2 Corinthians 4:8–10*

But you, beloved, building yourselves up on your most holy faith, praying in the Holy Spirit,

keep yourselves in the love of God, looking for the mercy of our Lord Jesus Christ unto eternal life.

*Jude 20–21*

For we walk by faith, not by sight.

*2 Corinthians 5:7*

Jesus said to him, "If you can believe, all things are possible to him who believes."

*Mark 9:23*

Whom have I in heaven but You?
And there is none upon earth that I desire besides You.
My flesh and my heart fail;
But God is the strength of my heart and my portion forever.

*Psalm 73:25–26*

Do not rejoice over me, my enemy;
When I fall, I will arise;

When I sit in darkness,
The LORD will be a light to me.

*Micah 7:8*

Behold the proud,
His soul is not upright in him;
But the just shall live by his faith.

*Habakkuk 2:4*

But someone will say, "You have faith, and I have works." Show me your faith without your works, and I will show you my faith by my works.

Do you see that faith was working together with his works, and by works faith was made perfect?

*James 2:18, 22*

Beloved, while I was very diligent to write to you concerning our common salvation, I found it necessary to write to you exhorting you to contend earnestly for the faith which was once for all delivered to the saints.

*Jude 3*

But recall the former days in which, after you were illuminated, you endured a great struggle with sufferings:

Therefore do not cast away your confidence, which has great reward.

For you have need of endurance, so that after you have done the will of God, you may receive the promise:

"For yet a little while,

And He who is coming will come and will not tarry.
Now the just shall live by faith;
But if anyone draws back,
My soul has no pleasure in him."
But we are not of those who draw back to perdition, but of those who believe to the saving of the soul.

*Hebrews 10:32, 35–39*

# Growing
## in Christ

# How to Overcome
# the Carnal Mind

For the law of the Spirit of life in Christ Jesus has made me free from the law of sin and death.

For what the law could not do in that it was weak through the flesh, God did by sending His own Son in the likeness of sinful flesh, on account of sin: He condemned sin in the flesh,

that the righteous requirement of the law might be fulfilled in us who do not walk according to the flesh but according to the Spirit.

For those who live according to the flesh set their minds on the things of the flesh, but those who live according to the Spirit, the things of the Spirit.

For to be carnally minded is death, but to be spiritually minded is life and peace.

Because the carnal mind is enmity against God; for it is not subject to the law of God, nor indeed can be.

So then, those who are in the flesh cannot please God.

But you are not in the flesh but in the Spirit, if indeed the Spirit of God dwells in you. Now if anyone does not have the Spirit of Christ, he is not His.

And if Christ is in you, the body is dead because of sin, but the Spirit is life because of righteousness.

But if the Spirit of Him who raised Jesus from the dead dwells in you, He who raised Christ from the dead will also give life to your mortal bodies through His Spirit who dwells in you.

Therefore, brethren, we are debtors—not to the flesh, to live according to the flesh.

For if you live according to the flesh you will die; but if by the Spirit you put to death the deeds of the body, you will live.

Yet in all these things we are more than conquerors through Him who loved us.

*Romans 8:2–13, 37*

For you, brethren, have been called to liberty; only do not use liberty as an opportunity for the flesh, but through love serve one another.

For all the law is fulfilled in one word, even in this: "You shall love your neighbor as yourself."

But if you bite and devour one another, beware lest you be consumed by one another!

I say then: Walk in the Spirit, and you shall not fulfill the lust of the flesh.

For the flesh lusts against the Spirit, and the Spirit against the flesh; and these are contrary to one another, so that you do not do the things that you wish.

*Galatians 5:13–17*

I beseech you therefore, brethren, by the mercies of God, that you present your bodies a living sacrifice, holy, acceptable to God, which is your reasonable service.

And do not be conformed to this world, but be transformed

by the renewing of your mind, that you may prove what is that good and acceptable and perfect will of God.

*Romans 12:1–2*

Therefore gird up the loins of your mind, be sober, and rest your hope fully upon the grace that is to be brought to you at the revelation of Jesus Christ;

as obedient children, not conforming yourselves to the former lusts, as in your ignorance;

but as He who called you is holy, you also be holy in all your conduct.

*1 Peter 1:13–15*

I have been crucified with Christ; it is no longer I who live, but Christ lives in me; and the life which I now live in the flesh I live by faith in the Son of God, who loved me and gave Himself for me.

*Galatians 2:20*

You will keep him in perfect peace,
Whose mind is stayed on You,
Because he trusts in You.

*Isaiah 26:3*

Knowing this, that our old man was crucified with Him, that the body of sin might be done away with, that we should no longer be slaves of sin.

Now if we died with Christ, we believe that we shall also live with Him, knowing that Christ, having been raised from the dead, dies no more. Death no longer has dominion over Him.

Likewise you also, reckon yourselves to be dead indeed to sin, but alive to God in Christ Jesus our Lord.

*Romans 6:6, 8–9, 11*


That you put off, concerning your former conduct, the old man which grows corrupt according to the deceitful lusts,

and be renewed in the spirit of your mind,

and that you put on the new man which was created according to God, in true righteousness and holiness.

*Ephesians 4:22–24*


Let this mind be in you which was also in Christ Jesus.

*Philippians 2:5*


Let us walk properly, as in the day, not in revelry and drunkenness, not in lewdness and lust, not in strife and envy.

But put on the Lord Jesus Christ, and make no provision for the flesh, to fulfill its lusts.

*Romans 13:13–14*


Therefore we do not lose heart. Even though our outward man is perishing, yet the inward man is being renewed day by day.

*2 Corinthians 4:16*

Beware lest anyone cheat you through philosophy and empty deceit, according to the tradition of men, according to the basic principles of the world, and not according to Christ.

*Colossians 2:8*


If your hand or foot causes you to sin, cut it off and cast it from you. It is better for you to enter into life lame or maimed, rather than having two hands or two feet, to be cast into the everlasting fire.

And if your eye causes you to sin, pluck it out and cast it from you. It is better for you to enter into life with one eye, rather than having two eyes, to be cast into hell fire.

*Matthew 18:8–9*


For "who has known the mind of the LORD that he may instruct Him?" But we have the mind of Christ.

*1 Corinthians 2:16*


For if there is first a willing mind, it is accepted according to what one has, and not according to what he does not have.

*2 Corinthians 8:12*


Whoever has no rule over his own spirit
Is like a city broken down, without walls.

*Proverbs 25:28*

Remember all the commandments of the Lord and do them, and that you may not follow the harlotry to which your own heart and your own eyes are inclined,

and that you may remember and do all My commandments, and be holy for your God.

*Numbers 15:39–40*

But what things were gain to me, these I have counted loss for Christ.

Yet indeed I also count all things loss for the excellence of the knowledge of Christ Jesus my Lord, for whom I have suffered the loss of all things, and count them as rubbish, that I may gain Christ.

*Philippians 3:7–8*

And those who are Christ's have crucified the flesh with its passions and desires.

If we live in the Spirit, let us also walk in the Spirit.

*Galatians 5:24–25*

But I discipline my body and bring it into subjection, lest, when I have preached to others, I myself should become disqualified.

*1 Corinthians 9:27*

There is a way that seems right to a man,
But its end is the way of death.

*Proverbs 14:12*

You cannot drink the cup of the Lord and the cup of demons; you cannot partake of the Lord's table and of the table of demons.

*1 Corinthians 10:21*

Finally, brethren, whatever things are true, whatever things are noble, whatever things are just, whatever things are pure, whatever things are lovely, whatever things are of good report, if there is any virtue and if there is anything praiseworthy—meditate on these things.

*Philippians 4:8*

# How to Overcome Satan

Finally, my brethren, be strong in the Lord and in the power of His might.

Put on the whole armor of God, that you may be able to stand against the wiles of the devil.

For we do not wrestle against flesh and blood, but against principalities, against powers, against the rulers of the darkness of this age, against spiritual hosts of wickedness in the heavenly places.

Therefore take up the whole armor of God, that you may be able to withstand in the evil day, and having done all, to stand.

Stand therefore, having girded your waist with truth, having put on the breastplate of righteousness,

and having shod your feet with the preparation of the gospel of peace;

above all, taking the shield of faith with which you will be able to quench all the fiery darts of the wicked one.

And take the helmet of salvation, and the sword of the Spirit, which is the word of God.

*Ephesians 6:10–17*

Therefore submit to God. Resist the devil and he will flee from you.

Draw near to God and He will draw near to you. Cleanse

your hands, you sinners; and purify your hearts, you double-minded.

*James 4:7–8*

And He said to them, "I saw Satan fall like lightning from heaven.

Behold, I give you the authority to trample on serpents and scorpions, and over all the power of the enemy, and nothing shall by any means hurt you."

*Luke 10:18–19*

Be sober, be vigilant; because your adversary the devil walks about like a roaring lion, seeking whom he may devour.

Resist him, steadfast in the faith, knowing that the same sufferings are experienced by your brotherhood in the world.

But may the God of all grace, who called us to His eternal glory by Christ Jesus, after you have suffered a while, perfect, establish, strengthen, and settle you.

*1 Peter 5:8–10*

The LORD shall preserve you from all evil;
He shall preserve your soul.
The LORD shall preserve your going out and your coming in
From this time forth, and even forevermore.

*Psalm 121:7–8*

Surely He shall deliver you from the snare of the fowler
And from the perilous pestilence.
He shall cover you with His feathers,

And under His wings you shall take refuge;
His truth shall be your shield and buckler.
You shall not be afraid of the terror by night,
Nor of the arrow that flies by day,
Nor of the pestilence that walks in darkness,
Nor of the destruction that lays waste at noonday.
A thousand may fall at your side,
And ten thousand at your right hand;
But it shall not come near you.

*Psalm 91:3–7*

He who sins is of the devil, for the devil has sinned from the beginning. For this purpose the Son of God was manifested, that He might destroy the works of the devil.

*1 John 3:8*

And the peace of God, which surpasses all understanding, will guard your hearts and minds through Christ Jesus.

Finally, brethren, whatever things are true, whatever things are noble, whatever things are just, whatever things are pure, whatever things are lovely, whatever things are of good report, if there is any virtue and if there is anything praiseworthy—meditate on these things.

*Philippians 4:7–8*

Beloved, do not believe every spirit, but test the spirits, whether they are of God; because many false prophets have gone out into the world.

By this you know the Spirit of God: Every spirit that confesses that Jesus Christ has come in the flesh is of God,

and every spirit that does not confess that Jesus Christ has come in the flesh is not of God. And this is the spirit of the Antichrist, which you have heard was coming, and is now already in the world.

You are of God, little children, and have overcome them, because He who is in you is greater than he who is in the world.

*1 John 4:1–4*


Now whom you forgive anything, I also forgive. For if indeed I have forgiven anything, I have forgiven that one for your sakes in the presence of Christ,

lest Satan should take advantage of us; for we are not ignorant of his devices.

*2 Corinthians 2:10–11*


"Be angry, and do not sin": do not let the sun go down on your wrath,

nor give place to the devil.

*Ephesians 4:26–27*


But the Lord is faithful, who will establish you and guard you from the evil one.

*2 Thessalonians 3:3*

And the Lord will deliver me from every evil work and preserve me for His heavenly kingdom. To Him be glory forever and ever. Amen!

*2 Timothy 4:18*

Yet in all these things we are more than conquerors through Him who loved us.

*Romans 8:37*

To him who overcomes I will grant to sit with Me on My throne, as I also overcame and sat down with My Father on His throne.

*Revelation 3:21*

The devil, who deceived them, was cast into the lake of fire and brimstone where the beast and the false prophet are. And they will be tormented day and night forever and ever.

*Revelation 20:10*

For in that He Himself has suffered, being tempted, He is able to aid those who are tempted.

*Hebrews 2:18*

But seek first the kingdom of God and His righteousness, and all these things shall be added to you.

Therefore do not worry about tomorrow, for tomorrow will worry about its own things. Sufficient for the day is its own trouble.

*Matthew 6:33–34*

Beware of false prophets, who come to you in sheep's clothing, but inwardly they are ravenous wolves.

You will know them by their fruits. Do men gather grapes from thornbushes or figs from thistles?

Even so, every good tree bears good fruit, but a bad tree bears bad fruit.

*Matthew 7:15–17*


Behold, I send you out as sheep in the midst of wolves. Therefore be wise as serpents and harmless as doves.

*Matthew 10:16*


Not a novice, lest being puffed up with pride he fall into the same condemnation as the devil.

Moreover he must have a good testimony among those who are outside, lest he fall into reproach and the snare of the devil.

*1 Timothy 3:6–7*

# How to Recognize Evil

Beware of false prophets, who come to you in sheep's clothing, but inwardly they are ravenous wolves.

You will know them by their fruits. Do men gather grapes from thornbushes or figs from thistles?

Even so, every good tree bears good fruit, but a bad tree bears bad fruit.

Therefore by their fruits you will know them.

Not everyone who says to Me, "Lord, Lord," shall enter the kingdom of heaven, but he who does the will of My Father in heaven.

Many will say to Me in that day, "Lord, Lord, have we not prophesied in Your name, cast out demons in Your name, and done many wonders in Your name?"

And then I will declare to them, "I never knew you; depart from Me, you who practice lawlessness!"

*Matthew 7:15–17, 20–23*

Beloved, do not believe every spirit, but test the spirits, whether they are of God; because many false prophets have gone out into the world.

By this you know the Spirit of God: Every spirit that confesses that Jesus Christ has come in the flesh is of God,

and every spirit that does not confess that Jesus Christ has come in the flesh is not of God. And this is the spirit of the Antichrist, which you have heard was coming, and is now already in the world.

*1 John 4:1–3*

And when they say to you, "Seek those who are mediums and wizards, who whisper and mutter," should not a people seek their God? Should they seek the dead on behalf of the living?

To the law and to the testimony! If they do not speak according to this word, it is because there is no light in them.

*Isaiah 8:19–20*

For God has not given us a spirit of fear, but of power and of love and of a sound mind.

*2 Timothy 1:7*

Stand fast therefore in the liberty by which Christ has made us free, and do not be entangled again with a yoke of bondage.

*Galatians 5:1*

"Behold, I am against those who prophesy false dreams," says the LORD, "and tell them, and cause My people to err by their lies and by their recklessness. Yet I did not send them or command them; therefore they shall not profit this people at all," says the LORD.

*Jeremiah 23:32*

For a good tree does not bear bad fruit, nor does a bad tree bear good fruit.

For every tree is known by its own fruit. For men do not gather figs from thorns, nor do they gather grapes from a bramble bush.

*Luke 6:43–44*


For God is not the author of confusion but of peace, as in all the churches of the saints.

*1 Corinthians 14:33*


A cunning Canaanite!
Deceitful scales are in his hand;
He loves to oppress.

*Hosea 12:7*


They profess to know God, but in works they deny Him, being abominable, disobedient, and disqualified for every good work.

*Titus 1:16*


He who sins is of the devil, for the devil has sinned from the beginning. For this purpose the Son of God was manifested, that He might destroy the works of the devil.

In this the children of God and the children of the devil are manifest: Whoever does not practice righteousness is not of God, nor is he who does not love his brother.

*1 John 3:8,10*

For many deceivers have gone out into the world who do not confess Jesus Christ as coming in the flesh. This is a deceiver and an antichrist.

Whoever transgresses and does not abide in the doctrine of Christ does not have God. He who abides in the doctrine of Christ has both the Father and the Son.

If anyone comes to you and does not bring this doctrine, do not receive him into your house nor greet him;

for he who greets him shares in his evil deeds.

*2 John 7, 9—11*

Desiring to be teachers of the law, understanding neither what they say nor the things which they affirm.

*1 Timothy 1:7*

His heart is as hard as stone,
Even as hard as the lower millstone.
He beholds every high thing;
He is king over all the children of pride.

*Job 41:24, 34*

Whom will he teach knowledge?
And whom will he make to understand the message?
Those just weaned from milk?
Those just drawn from the breasts?

*Isaiah 28:9*

And you shall take no bribe, for a bribe blinds the discerning and perverts the words of the righteous.

*Exodus 23:8*

For certain men have crept in unnoticed, who long ago were marked out for this condemnation, ungodly men, who turn the grace of our God into lewdness and deny the only Lord God and our Lord Jesus Christ.

*Jude 4*

# HOW TO OVERCOME WORLDLINESS

No one can serve two masters; for either he will hate the one and love the other, or else he will be loyal to the one and despise the other. You cannot serve God and mammon.

*Matthew 6:24*

Do not love the world or the things in the world. If anyone loves the world, the love of the Father is not in him.

For all that is in the world—the lust of the flesh, the lust of the eyes, and the pride of life—is not of the Father but is of the world.

And the world is passing away, and the lust of it; but he who does the will of God abides forever.

*1 John 2:15–17*

And do not be conformed to this world, but be transformed by the renewing of your mind, that you may prove what is that good and acceptable and perfect will of God.

*Romans 12:2*

And do this, knowing the time, that now it is high time to awake out of sleep; for now our salvation is nearer than when we first believed.

The night is far spent, the day is at hand. Therefore let us cast off the works of darkness, and let us put on the armor of light.

Let us walk properly, as in the day, not in revelry and drunkenness, not in lewdness and lust, not in strife and envy.

But put on the Lord Jesus Christ, and make no provision for the flesh, to fulfill its lusts.

*Romans 13:11—14*

And have no fellowship with the unfruitful works of darkness, but rather expose them.

*Ephesians 5:11*

Then the Lord knows how to deliver the godly out of temptations and to reserve the unjust under punishment for the day of judgment.

*2 Peter 2:9*

Then He said to them all, "If anyone desires to come after Me, let him deny himself, and take up his cross daily, and follow Me.

For whoever desires to save his life will lose it, but whoever loses his life for My sake will save it.

For what profit is it to a man if he gains the whole world, and is himself destroyed or lost?"

*Luke 9:23—25*

Now therefore, fear the LORD, serve Him in sincerity and in truth, and put away the gods which your fathers served on the other side of the River and in Egypt. Serve the LORD!

*Joshua 24:14*

Choosing rather to suffer affliction with the people of God than to enjoy the passing pleasures of sin,

esteeming the reproach of Christ greater riches than the treasures in Egypt; for he looked to the reward.

By faith he forsook Egypt, not fearing the wrath of the king; for he endured as seeing Him who is invisible.

*Hebrews 11:25–27*

By which have been given to us exceedingly great and precious promises, that through these you may be partakers of the divine nature, having escaped the corruption that is in the world through lust.

*2 Peter 1:4*

But take heed to yourselves, lest your hearts be weighed down with carousing, drunkenness, and cares of this life, and that Day come on you unexpectedly.

*Luke 21:34*

Set your mind on things above, not on things on the earth.

Do not lie to one another, since you have put off the old man with his deeds,

and have put on the new man who is renewed in knowledge according to the image of Him who created him.

*Colossians 3:2, 9–10*

No temptation has overtaken you except such as is common to man; but God is faithful, who will not allow you to be tempted beyond what you are able, but with the temptation will also make the way of escape, that you may be able to bear it.

You cannot drink the cup of the Lord and the cup of demons; you cannot partake of the Lord's table and of the table of demons.

*1 Corinthians 10:13, 21*

But we have renounced the hidden things of shame, not walking in craftiness nor handling the word of God deceitfully, but by manifestation of the truth commending ourselves to every man's conscience in the sight of God.

*2 Corinthians 4:2*

Teaching us that, denying ungodliness and worldly lusts, we should live soberly, righteously, and godly in the present age,

looking for the blessed hope and glorious appearing of our great God and Savior Jesus Christ.

*Titus 2:12–13*

But what things were gain to me, these I have counted loss for Christ.

*Philippians 3:7*

Who is he who overcomes the world, but he who believes that Jesus is the Son of God?

*1 John 5:5*

So then, my beloved brethren, let every man be swift to hear, slow to speak, slow to wrath;

for the wrath of man does not produce the righteousness of God.

Therefore lay aside all filthiness and overflow of wickedness, and receive with meekness the implanted word, which is able to save your souls.

Pure and undefiled religion before God and the Father is this: to visit orphans and widows in their trouble, and to keep oneself unspotted from the world.

*James 1:19–21, 27*


And He said to them, "Take heed and beware of covetousness, for one's life does not consist in the abundance of the things he possesses."

*Luke 12:15*


Out of the same mouth proceed blessing and cursing. My brethren, these things ought not to be so.

Does a spring send forth fresh water and bitter from the same opening?

*James 3:10–11*


Adulterers and adulteresses! Do you not know that friendship with the world is enmity with God? Whoever therefore wants to be a friend of the world makes himself an enemy of God.

*James 4:4*

These things I have spoken to you, that in Me you may have peace. In the world you will have tribulation; but be of good cheer, I have overcome the world.

*John 16:33*

Wine is a mocker,
Strong drink is a brawler,
And whoever is led astray by it is not wise.

*Proverbs 20:1*

Hell and Destruction are never full;
So the eyes of man are never satisfied.

*Proverbs 27:20*

"Woe to the rebellious children," says the LORD,
"Who take counsel, but not of Me,
And who devise plans, but not of My Spirit,
That they may add sin to sin."

*Isaiah 30:1*

Likewise you also, reckon yourselves to be dead indeed to sin, but alive to God in Christ Jesus our Lord.

Therefore do not let sin reign in your mortal body, that you should obey it in its lusts.

*Romans 6:11–12*

Do not be unequally yoked together with unbelievers. For what fellowship has righteousness with lawlessness? And what communion has light with darkness?

And what accord has Christ with Belial? Or what part has a believer with an unbeliever?

And what agreement has the temple of God with idols? For you are the temple of the living God. As God has said:

"I will dwell in them
And walk among them.
I will be their God,
And they shall be My people."
Therefore
"Come out from among them
And be separate, says the Lord.
Do not touch what is unclean,
And I will receive you."

*2 Corinthians 6:14–17*

Now these are the ones sown among thorns; they are the ones who hear the word,

and the cares of this world, the deceitfulness of riches, and the desires for other things entering in choke the word, and it becomes unfruitful.

But these are the ones sown on good ground, those who hear the word, accept it, and bear fruit: some thirtyfold, some sixty, and some a hundred.

*Mark 4:18–20*

# How to Deal with Lust

Do you not know that your bodies are members of Christ? Shall I then take the members of Christ and make them members of a harlot? Certainly not!

Or do you not know that he who is joined to a harlot is one body with her? For "the two," He says, "shall become one flesh."

But he who is joined to the Lord is one spirit with Him.

Flee sexual immorality. Every sin that a man does is outside the body, but he who commits sexual immorality sins against his own body.

Or do you not know that your body is the temple of the Holy Spirit who is in you, whom you have from God, and you are not your own?

For you were bought at a price; therefore glorify God in your body and in your spirit, which are God's.

*1 Corinthians 6:15–20*

I say then: Walk in the Spirit, and you shall not fulfill the lust of the flesh.

For the flesh lusts against the Spirit, and the Spirit against the flesh; and these are contrary to one another, so that you do not do the things that you wish.

*Galatians 5:16–17*

No temptation has overtaken you except such as is common to man; but God is faithful, who will not allow you to be tempted beyond what you are able, but with the temptation will also make the way of escape, that you may be able to bear it.

*1 Corinthians 10:13*

That you put off, concerning your former conduct, the old man which grows corrupt according to the deceitful lusts,
and be renewed in the spirit of your mind,
and that you put on the new man which was created according to God, in true righteousness and holiness . . .
nor give place to the devil.

*Ephesians 4:22–24, 27*

Therefore submit to God. Resist the devil and he will flee from you.

*James 4:7*

Do not lust after her beauty in your heart,
Nor let her allure you with her eyelids.
For by means of a harlot
A man is reduced to a crust of bread;
And an adulteress will prey upon his precious life.

*Proverbs 6:25–26*

Now therefore, listen to me, my children;
Pay attention to the words of my mouth:
Do not let your heart turn aside to her ways,
Do not stray into her paths;

For she has cast down many wounded,
And all who were slain by her were strong men.
Her house is the way to hell,
Descending to the chambers of death.

*Proverbs 7:24–27*

Then the Lord knows how to deliver the godly out of temptations and to reserve the unjust under punishment for the day of judgment.

*2 Peter 2:9*

My brethren, count it all joy when you fall into various trials,
knowing that the testing of your faith produces patience.
But let patience have its perfect work, that you may be perfect and complete, lacking nothing.

*James 1:2–4*

For we do not have a High Priest who cannot sympathize with our weaknesses, but was in all points tempted as we are, yet without sin.

*Hebrews 4:15*

For the weapons of our warfare are not carnal but mighty in God for pulling down strongholds.

*2 Corinthians 10:4*

He who is greedy for gain troubles his own house,
But he who hates bribes will live.

The LORD is far from the wicked,
But He hears the prayer of the righteous.

*Proverbs 15:27, 29*

So they came to Jerusalem. Then Jesus went into the temple and began to drive out those who bought and sold in the temple, and overturned the tables of the money changers and the seats of those who sold doves.

Then He taught, saying to them, "Is it not written, 'My house shall be called a house of prayer for all nations'? But you have made it a 'den of thieves.'"

*Mark 11:15, 17*

A man with an evil eye hastens after riches,
And does not consider that poverty will come upon him.

*Proverbs 28:22*

For riches are not forever,
Nor does a crown endure to all generations.

*Proverbs 27:24*

For in that day every man shall throw away his idols of silver and his idols of gold—sin, which your own hands have made for yourselves.

*Isaiah 31:7*

If your hand or foot causes you to sin, cut it off and cast it from you. It is better for you to enter into life lame or maimed, rather than having two hands or two feet, to be cast into the everlasting fire.

And if your eye causes you to sin, pluck it out and cast it from you. It is better for you to enter into life with one eye, rather than having two eyes, to be cast into hell fire.

*Matthew 18:8–9*

But with most of them God was not well pleased, for their bodies were scattered in the wilderness.

Now these things became our examples, to the intent that we should not lust after evil things as they also lusted.

And do not become idolaters as were some of them. As it is written, "The people sat down to eat and drink, and rose up to play."

Nor let us commit sexual immorality, as some of them did, and in one day twenty-three thousand fell.

*1 Corinthians 10:5–8*

For this you know, that no fornicator, unclean person, nor covetous man, who is an idolater, has any inheritance in the kingdom of Christ and God.

Therefore do not be partakers with them.

For you were once darkness, but now you are light in the Lord. Walk as children of light

(for the fruit of the Spirit is in all goodness, righteousness, and truth) . . .

And do not be drunk with wine, in which is dissipation; but be filled with the Spirit.

*Ephesians 5:5, 7–9, 18*

# How to Overcome Pride

Pride goes before destruction,
And a haughty spirit before a fall.
Better to be of a humble spirit with the lowly,
Than to divide the spoil with the proud.
He who heeds the word wisely will find good,
And whoever trusts in the LORD, happy is he.

*Proverbs 16:18–20*

He who is of a proud heart stirs up strife,
But he who trusts in the LORD will be prospered.
He who trusts in his own heart is a fool,
But whoever walks wisely will be delivered.

*Proverbs 28:25–26*

Then Jesus called a little child to Him, set him in the midst of them,

and said, "Assuredly, I say to you, unless you are converted and become as little children, you will by no means enter the kingdom of heaven.

Therefore whoever humbles himself as this little child is the greatest in the kingdom of heaven."

*Matthew 18:2–4*

But He gives more grace.

Therefore He says:

"God resists the proud,

But gives grace to the humble."

Therefore submit to God. Resist the devil and he will flee from you.

Humble yourselves in the sight of the Lord, and He will lift you up.

*James 4:6–7, 10*


Yet it shall not be so among you; but whoever desires to become great among you, let him be your servant.

And whoever desires to be first among you, let him be your slave.

*Matthew 20:26–27*


Likewise you younger people, submit yourselves to your elders. Yes, all of you be submissive to one another, and be clothed with humility, for

"God resists the proud,

But gives grace to the humble."

Therefore humble yourselves under the mighty hand of God, that He may exalt you in due time.

*1 Peter 5:5–6*


Hear and give ear:

Do not be proud,

For the LORD has spoken.

Give glory to the LORD your God

Before He causes darkness,
And before your feet stumble
On the dark mountains,
And while you are looking for light,
He turns it into the shadow of death
And makes it dense darkness.
But if you will not hear it,
My soul will weep in secret for your pride;
My eyes will weep bitterly
And run down with tears,
Because the LORD's flock has been taken captive.

*Jeremiah 13:15–17*


Take My yoke upon you and learn from Me, for I am gentle and lowly in heart, and you will find rest for your souls.
For My yoke is easy and My burden is light.

*Matthew 11:29–30*


The fear of the LORD is the instruction of wisdom,
And before honor is humility.

*Proverbs 15:33*


And whoever of you desires to be first shall be slave of all.

*Mark 10:44*


But we have this treasure in earthen vessels, that the excellence of the power may be of God and not of us.

*2 Corinthians 4:7*

But "he who glories, let him glory in the LORD."

For not he who commends himself is approved, but whom the Lord commends.

2 Corinthians 10:17–18

By humility and the fear of the LORD
Are riches and honor and life.

Proverbs 22:4

Do not boast about tomorrow,
For you do not know what a day may bring forth.
Let another man praise you, and not your own mouth;
A stranger, and not your own lips.

Proverbs 27:1–2

A man's pride will bring him low,
But the humble in spirit will retain honor.

Proverbs 29:23

Before destruction the heart of a man is haughty,
And before honor is humility.

Proverbs 18:12

Better a poor and wise youth
Than an old and foolish king who will be admonished no more.

Ecclesiastes 4:13

Not a novice, lest being puffed up with pride he fall into the same condemnation as the devil.

Moreover he must have a good testimony among those who are outside, lest he fall into reproach and the snare of the devil.

*1 Timothy 3:6–7*

But he who is greatest among you shall be your servant.

And whoever exalts himself will be humbled, and he who humbles himself will be exalted.

*Matthew 23:11–12*

The Pharisee stood and prayed thus with himself, "God, I thank You that I am not like other men—extortioners, unjust, adulterers, or even as this tax collector.

I fast twice a week; I give tithes of all that I possess."

And the tax collector, standing afar off, would not so much as raise his eyes to heaven, but beat his breast, saying, "God, be merciful to me a sinner!"

I tell you, this man went down to his house justified rather than the other; for everyone who exalts himself will be humbled, and he who humbles himself will be exalted.

*Luke 18:11–14*

Though the LORD is on high,
Yet He regards the lowly;
But the proud He knows from afar.

*Psalm 138:6*

# How to Control Your Tongue

Death and life are in the power of the tongue,
And those who love it will eat its fruit.

*Proverbs 18:21*

Let no corrupt word proceed out of your mouth, but what is good for necessary edification, that it may impart grace to the hearers.

Let all bitterness, wrath, anger, clamor, and evil speaking be put away from you, with all malice.

And be kind to one another, tenderhearted, forgiving one another, even as God in Christ forgave you.

*Ephesians 4:29, 31–32*

Pleasant words are like a honeycomb,
Sweetness to the soul and health to the bones.

*Proverbs 16:24*

He who guards his mouth preserves his life,
But he who opens wide his lips shall have destruction.

*Proverbs 13:3*

A good man out of the good treasure of his heart brings forth good; and an evil man out of the evil treasure of his heart brings forth evil. For out of the abundance of the heart his mouth speaks.

*Luke 6:45*

But I say to you that for every idle word men may speak, they will give account of it in the day of judgment.

*Matthew 12:36*

Sing to Him, sing psalms to Him;
Talk of all His wondrous works!

*1 Chronicles 16:9*

Whoever guards his mouth and tongue
Keeps his soul from troubles.

*Proverbs 21:23*

Do not be a witness against your neighbor without cause,
For would you deceive with your lips?

*Proverbs 24:28*

O Timothy! Guard what was committed to your trust, avoiding the profane and idle babblings and contradictions of what is falsely called knowledge—
by professing it some have strayed concerning the faith. Grace be with you. Amen.

*1 Timothy 6:20–21*

But avoid foolish disputes, genealogies, contentions, and strivings about the law; for they are unprofitable and useless.

*Titus 3:9*


As long as my breath is in me,
And the breath of God in my nostrils,
My lips will not speak wickedness,
Nor my tongue utter deceit.

*Job 27:3–4*


But he said to her, "You speak as one of the foolish women speaks. Shall we indeed accept good from God, and shall we not accept adversity?" In all this Job did not sin with his lips.

*Job 2:10*


For
"He who would love life
And see good days,
Let him refrain his tongue from evil,
And his lips from speaking deceit."

*1 Peter 3:10*


But as He who called you is holy, you also be holy in all your conduct.

*1 Peter 1:15*

Who, when He was reviled, did not revile in return; when He suffered, He did not threaten, but committed Himself to Him who judges righteously.

*1 Peter 2:23*

A wholesome tongue is a tree of life,
But perverseness in it breaks the spirit.

*Proverbs 15:4*

A fool's mouth is his destruction,
And his lips are the snare of his soul.
The words of a talebearer are like tasty trifles,
And they go down into the inmost body.

*Proverbs 18:7–8*

And the tongue is a fire, a world of iniquity. The tongue is so set among our members that it defiles the whole body, and sets on fire the course of nature; and it is set on fire by hell.

Out of the same mouth proceed blessing and cursing. My brethren, these things ought not to be so.

Does a spring send forth fresh water and bitter from the same opening?

*James 3:6, 10–11*

If anyone among you thinks he is religious, and does not bridle his tongue but deceives his own heart, this one's religion is useless.

*James 1:26*

Concerning the works of men,
By the word of Your lips,
I have kept away from the paths of the destroyer.

*Psalm 17:4*


There is one who speaks like the piercings of a sword,
But the tongue of the wise promotes health.
The truthful lip shall be established forever,
But a lying tongue is but for a moment.

*Proverbs 12:18–19*


Set a guard, O LORD, over my mouth;
Keep watch over the door of my lips.

*Psalm 141:3*


There is gold and a multitude of rubies,
But the lips of knowledge are a precious jewel.

*Proverbs 20:15*

# How to Be Christ-Centered

Let the word of Christ dwell in you richly in all wisdom, teaching and admonishing one another in psalms and hymns and spiritual songs, singing with grace in your hearts to the Lord.

And whatever you do in word or deed, do all in the name of the Lord Jesus, giving thanks to God the Father through Him.

*Colossians 3:16–17*

I love those who love Me,
And those who seek Me diligently will find Me.

*Proverbs 8:17*

Seek the LORD and His strength;
Seek His face evermore!
Remember His marvelous works which He has done,
His wonders, and the judgments of His mouth.

*1 Chronicles 16:11–12*

You are My friends if you do whatever I command you.

No longer do I call you servants, for a servant does not know what his master is doing; but I have called you friends, for all things that I heard from My Father I have made known to you.

You did not choose Me, but I chose you and appointed you that you should go and bear fruit, and that your fruit should remain, that whatever you ask the Father in My name He may give you.

*John 15:14–16*

Speaking to one another in psalms and hymns and spiritual songs, singing and making melody in your heart to the Lord,
giving thanks always for all things to God the Father in the name of our Lord Jesus Christ.

*Ephesians 5:19–20*

I will bless the LORD at all times;
His praise shall continually be in my mouth.
My soul shall make its boast in the LORD;
The humble shall hear of it and be glad.
Oh, magnify the LORD with me,
And let us exalt His name together.
I sought the LORD, and He heard me,
And delivered me from all my fears.

*Psalm 34:1–4*

O God, You are my God;
Early will I seek You;
My soul thirsts for You;
My flesh longs for You
In a dry and thirsty land
Where there is no water.
So I have looked for You in the sanctuary,

To see Your power and Your glory.
My soul shall be satisfied as with marrow and fatness,
And my mouth shall praise You with joyful lips.
When I remember You on my bed,
I meditate on You in the night watches.
Because You have been my help,
Therefore in the shadow of Your wings I will rejoice.

*Psalm 63:1–2, 5–7*

But put on the Lord Jesus Christ, and make no provision
for the flesh, to fulfill its lusts.

*Romans 13:14*

So I will sing praise to Your name forever,
That I may daily perform my vows.

*Psalm 61:8*

In You, O LORD, I put my trust;
Let me never be put to shame.
For You are my hope, O Lord GOD;
You are my trust from my youth.
Let my mouth be filled with Your praise
And with Your glory all the day.

*Psalm 71:1, 5, 8*

Trust in Him at all times, you people;
Pour out your heart before Him;
God is a refuge for us. Selah

*Psalm 62:8*

Let them shout for joy and be glad,
Who favor my righteous cause;
And let them say continually,
"Let the LORD be magnified,
Who has pleasure in the prosperity of His servant."
And my tongue shall speak of Your righteousness
And of Your praise all the day long.

*Psalm 35:27–28*


It is good to give thanks to the LORD,
And to sing praises to Your name, O Most High;
To declare Your lovingkindness in the morning,
And Your faithfulness every night,
For You, LORD, have made me glad through Your work;
I will triumph in the works of Your hands.

*Psalm 92:1–2, 4*


Sing to the LORD, bless His name;
Proclaim the good news of His salvation from day to day.

*Psalm 96:2*


From the rising of the sun to its going down
The LORD's name is to be praised.

*Psalm 113:3*


I will delight myself in Your statutes;
I will not forget Your word.

Make me understand the way of Your precepts;
So shall I meditate on Your wonderful works.

*Psalm 119:16, 27*


My soul waits for the Lord
More than those who watch for the morning—
Yes, more than those who watch for the morning.
O Israel, hope in the LORD;
For with the LORD there is mercy,
And with Him is abundant redemption.

*Psalm 130:6–7*


I will sing to the LORD as long as I live;
I will sing praise to my God while I have my being.
May my meditation be sweet to Him;
I will be glad in the LORD.

*Psalm 104:33–34*


Therefore by Him let us continually offer the sacrifice of praise to God, that is, the fruit of our lips, giving thanks to His name.

*Hebrews 13:15*


You will keep him in perfect peace,
Whose mind is stayed on You,
Because he trusts in You.

*Isaiah 26:3*

Then He said to them all, "If anyone desires to come after Me, let him deny himself, and take up his cross daily, and follow Me.

For whoever desires to save his life will lose it, but whoever loses his life for My sake will save it.

For what profit is it to a man if he gains the whole world, and is himself destroyed or lost?"

*Luke 9:23–25*

# How to Understand
# the Liberty That Is in Christ

There is therefore now no condemnation to those who are in Christ Jesus, who do not walk according to the flesh, but according to the Spirit.

For the law of the Spirit of life in Christ Jesus has made me free from the law of sin and death.

*Romans 8:1–2*

For you, brethren, have been called to liberty; only do not use liberty as an opportunity for the flesh, but through love serve one another.

*Galatians 5:13*

There is neither Jew nor Greek, there is neither slave nor free, there is neither male nor female; for you are all one in Christ Jesus.

*Galatians 3:28*

But he who looks into the perfect law of liberty and continues in it, and is not a forgetful hearer but a doer of the work, this one will be blessed in what he does.

*James 1:25*

"I, Jesus, have sent My angel to testify to you these things in the churches. I am the Root and the Offspring of David, the Bright and Morning Star."

And the Spirit and the bride say, "Come!" And let him who hears say, "Come!" And let him who thirsts come. Whoever desires, let him take the water of life freely.

*Revelation 22:16–17*

And you shall know the truth, and the truth shall make you free.

Therefore if the Son makes you free, you shall be free indeed.

*John 8:32, 36*

Now the Lord is the Spirit; and where the Spirit of the Lord is, there is liberty.

*2 Corinthians 3:17*

Stand fast therefore in the liberty by which Christ has made us free, and do not be entangled again with a yoke of bondage.

*Galatians 5:1*

Because the creation itself also will be delivered from the bondage of corruption into the glorious liberty of the children of God.

*Romans 8:21*

Am I not an apostle? Am I not free? Have I not seen Jesus Christ our Lord? Are you not my work in the Lord?

*1 Corinthians 9:1*

As free, yet not using liberty as a cloak for vice, but as bondservants of God.

*1 Peter 2:16*

Even the righteousness of God, through faith in Jesus Christ, to all and on all who believe. For there is no difference;
for all have sinned and fall short of the glory of God,
being justified freely by His grace through the redemption that is in Christ Jesus,
whom God set forth as a propitiation by His blood, through faith, to demonstrate His righteousness, because in His forbearance God had passed over the sins that were previously committed.

*Romans 3:22—25*

For thus says the LORD:
"You have sold yourselves for nothing,
And you shall be redeemed without money."

*Isaiah 52:3*

# HOW TO PRAISE THE LORD

Because Your lovingkindness is better than life,
My lips shall praise You.
Thus I will bless You while I live;
I will lift up my hands in Your name.
My soul shall be satisfied as with marrow and fatness,
And my mouth shall praise You with joyful lips.

*Psalm 63:3–5*

Praise the LORD!
Sing to the LORD a new song,
And His praise in the assembly of saints.
Let Israel rejoice in their Maker;
Let the children of Zion be joyful in their King.
Let them praise His name with the dance;
Let them sing praises to Him with the timbrel and harp.
For the LORD takes pleasure in His people;
He will beautify the humble with salvation.
Let the saints be joyful in glory;
Let them sing aloud on their beds.
Let the high praises of God be in their mouth,
And a two-edged sword in their hand.

*Psalm 149:1–6*

Praise the LORD! Praise God in His sanctuary;
Praise Him in His mighty firmament!
Praise Him for His mighty acts;
Praise Him according to His excellent greatness!
Praise Him with the sound of the trumpet;
Praise Him with the lute and harp!
Praise Him with the timbrel and dance;
Praise Him with stringed instruments and flutes!
Praise Him with loud cymbals;
Praise Him with clashing cymbals!
Let everything that has breath praise the LORD.
Praise the LORD!

*Psalm 150:1–6*

I will bless the LORD at all times;
His praise shall continually be in my mouth.

*Psalm 34:1*

Praise the LORD!
Praise, O servants of the LORD,
Praise the name of the LORD!
Blessed be the name of the LORD
From this time forth and forevermore!
From the rising of the sun to its going down
The LORD's name is to be praised.

*Psalm 113:1–3*

Whoever offers praise glorifies Me;
And to him who orders his conduct aright
I will show the salvation of God.

*Psalm 50:23*


Let your conduct be without covetousness; be content with such things as you have. For He Himself has said, "I will never leave you nor forsake you."

*Hebrews 13:5*


"The voice of joy and the voice of gladness, the voice of the bridegroom and the voice of the bride, the voice of those who will say:

'Praise the LORD of hosts,
For the LORD is good,
For His mercy endures forever'—

and of those who will bring the sacrifice of praise into the house of the LORD. For I will cause the captives of the land to return as at the first," says the LORD.

*Jeremiah 33:11*


But you are a chosen generation, a royal priesthood, a holy nation, His own special people, that you may proclaim the praises of Him who called you out of darkness into His marvelous light.

*1 Peter 2:9*


Accept, I pray, the freewill offerings of my mouth,
O LORD,

And teach me Your judgments.

*Psalm 119:108*

But at midnight Paul and Silas were praying and singing hymns to God, and the prisoners were listening to them.

*Acts 16:25*

Praise the LORD!
Praise the LORD, O my soul!
While I live I will praise the LORD;
I will sing praises to my God while I have my being.

*Psalm 146:1–2*

Oh, that men would give thanks to the LORD for His goodness,
    And for His wonderful works to the children of men!
    Let them sacrifice the sacrifices of thanksgiving,
    And declare His works with rejoicing.

*Psalm 107:21–22*

My heart is steadfast, O God, my heart is steadfast;
I will sing and give praise.
Awake, my glory!
Awake, lute and harp!
I will awaken the dawn.
I will praise You, O Lord, among the peoples;
I will sing to You among the nations.

*Psalm 57:7–9*

Great is the LORD, and greatly to be praised
In the city of our God,
In His holy mountain.

*Psalm 48:1*

I will praise the name of God with a song,
And will magnify Him with thanksgiving.

*Psalm 69:30*

He who believes in Me, as the Scripture has said, out of his heart will flow rivers of living water.

*John 7:38*

# HOW TO HAVE THE JOY
## OF THE LORD

His lord said to him, "Well done, good and faithful servant; you were faithful over a few things, I will make you ruler over many things. Enter into the joy of your lord."

*Matthew 25:21*

These things I have spoken to you, that My joy may remain in you, and that your joy may be full.

This is My commandment, that you love one another as I have loved you.

*John 15:11–12*

But let all those rejoice who put their trust in You
Let them ever shout for joy, because You defend them;
Let those also who love Your name
Be joyful in You.
For You, O LORD, will bless the righteous;
With favor You will surround him as with a shield.

*Psalm 5:11–12*

Come to Me, all you who labor and are heavy laden, and I will give you rest.

Take My yoke upon you and learn from Me, for I am gentle

and lowly in heart, and you will find rest for your souls.

For My yoke is easy and My burden is light.

*Matthew 11:28–30*


For God has not given us a spirit of fear, but of power and of love and of a sound mind.

*2 Timothy 1:7*


For the kingdom of God is not eating and drinking, but righteousness and peace and joy in the Holy Spirit.

For he who serves Christ in these things is acceptable to God and approved by men.

*Romans 14:17–18*


A merry heart does good, like medicine,
But a broken spirit dries the bones.

*Proverbs 17:22*


Nevertheless do not rejoice in this, that the spirits are subject to you, but rather rejoice because your names are written in heaven.

In that hour Jesus rejoiced in the Spirit and said, "I thank You, Father, Lord of heaven and earth, that You have hidden these things from the wise and prudent and revealed them to babes. Even so, Father, for so it seemed good in Your sight."

*Luke 10:20–21*


You love righteousness and hate wickedness;
Therefore God, Your God, has anointed You

With the oil of gladness more than Your companions.

All Your garments are scented with myrrh and aloes and cassia,

Out of the ivory palaces, by which they have made You glad.

*Psalm 45:7–8*

A merry heart makes a cheerful countenance,
But by sorrow of the heart the spirit is broken.

*Proverbs 15:13*

And you became followers of us and of the Lord, having received the word in much affliction, with joy of the Holy Spirit.

*1 Thessalonians 1:6*

Restore to me the joy of Your salvation,
And uphold me by Your generous Spirit.
Then I will teach transgressors Your ways,
And sinners shall be converted to You.

*Psalm 51:12–13*

Let the saints be joyful in glory;
Let them sing aloud on their beds.

*Psalm 149:5*

This is the day the LORD has made;
We will rejoice and be glad in it.

*Psalm 118:24*

Those who sow in tears
Shall reap in joy.
He who continually goes forth weeping,
Bearing seed for sowing,
Shall doubtless come again with rejoicing,
Bringing his sheaves with him.

*Psalm 126:5–6*


For this day is holy to our Lord. Do not sorrow, for the joy of the LORD is your strength.

*Nehemiah 8:10*

# Maturing
## in Christ

# HOW TO HANDLE SPIRITUAL TRIALS

Beloved, do not think it strange concerning the fiery trial which is to try you, as though some strange thing happened to you;

but rejoice to the extent that you partake of Christ's sufferings, that when His glory is revealed, you may also be glad with exceeding joy.

Yet if anyone suffers as a Christian, let him not be ashamed, but let him glorify God in this matter.

*1 Peter 4:12–13, 16*

When you pass through the waters, I will be with you;
And through the rivers, they shall not overflow you.
When you walk through the fire, you shall not be burned,
Nor shall the flame scorch you.
For I am the LORD your God,
The Holy One of Israel, your Savior;
I gave Egypt for your ransom,
Ethiopia and Seba in your place.

*Isaiah 43:2–3*

Deliver me out of the mire,
And let me not sink;
Let me be delivered from those who hate me,

And out of the deep waters.
Let not the floodwater overflow me,
Nor let the deep swallow me up;
And let not the pit shut its mouth on me.
Hear me, O LORD, for Your lovingkindness is good;
Turn to me according to the multitude of Your tender
mercies.
And do not hide Your face from Your servant,
For I am in trouble;
Hear me speedily.
Draw near to my soul, and redeem it;
Deliver me because of my enemies.

*Psalm 69:14—18*

In You, O LORD, I put my trust;
Let me never be ashamed;
Deliver me in Your righteousness.
Bow down Your ear to me,
Deliver me speedily;
Be my rock of refuge,
A fortress of defense to save me.
For You are my rock and my fortress;
Therefore, for Your name's sake,
Lead me and guide me.
Pull me out of the net which they have secretly laid for me,
For You are my strength.
Into Your hand I commit my spirit;
You have redeemed me,
O LORD God of truth.

I will be glad and rejoice in Your mercy,
For You have considered my trouble;
You have known my soul in adversities,
And have not shut me up into the hand of the enemy;
You have set my feet in a wide place.

*Psalm 31:1–5, 7–8*


The righteous cry out, and the LORD hears,
And delivers them out of all their troubles.
The LORD is near to those who have a broken heart,
And saves such as have a contrite spirit.
Many are the afflictions of the righteous,
But the LORD delivers him out of them all.

*Psalm 34:17–19*


For You will light my lamp;
The LORD my God will enlighten my darkness.
For by You I can run against a troop,
By my God I can leap over a wall.
As for God, His way is perfect;
The word of the LORD is proven;
He is a shield to all who trust in Him.
It is God who arms me with strength,
And makes my way perfect.

*Psalm 18:28–30, 32*


Why are you cast down, O my soul?
And why are you disquieted within me?
Hope in God;

For I shall yet praise Him,
The help of my countenance and my God.

*Psalm 43:5*


All this has come upon us;
But we have not forgotten You,
Nor have we dealt falsely with Your covenant.
Our heart has not turned back,
Nor have our steps departed from Your way;
But You have severely broken us in the place of jackals,
And covered us with the shadow of death.
If we had forgotten the name of our God,
Or stretched out our hands to a foreign god,
Would not God search this out?
For He knows the secrets of the heart.

*Psalm 44:17–21*


Cast your burden on the LORD,
And He shall sustain you;
He shall never permit the righteous to be moved.

*Psalm 55:22*


Create in me a clean heart, O God,
And renew a steadfast spirit within me.
Do not cast me away from Your presence,
And do not take Your Holy Spirit from me.
Restore to me the joy of Your salvation,
And uphold me by Your generous Spirit.
The sacrifices of God are a broken spirit,

A broken and a contrite heart—
These, O God, You will not despise.

*Psalm 51:10–12, 17*


Give us help from trouble,
For the help of man is useless.
Through God we will do valiantly,
For it is He who shall tread down our enemies.

*Psalm 60:11–12*


In God I have put my trust;
I will not be afraid.
What can man do to me?
Vows made to You are binding upon me, O God;
I will render praises to You,
For You have delivered my soul from death.
Have You not kept my feet from falling,
That I may walk before God
In the light of the living?

*Psalm 56:11–13*


I will extol You, O LORD, for You have lifted me up,
And have not let my foes rejoice over me.
O LORD my God, I cried out to You,
And You healed me.
O LORD, You brought my soul up from the grave;
You have kept me alive, that I should not go down to the pit.
Sing praise to the LORD, you saints of His,
And give thanks at the remembrance of His holy name.

For His anger is but for a moment,
His favor is for life;
Weeping may endure for a night,
But joy comes in the morning.

*Psalm 30:1–5*

The LORD has chastened me severely,
But He has not given me over to death.
Open to me the gates of righteousness;
I will go through them,
And I will praise the LORD.
This is the gate of the LORD,
Through which the righteous shall enter.
I will praise You,
For You have answered me,
And have become my salvation.

*Psalm 118:18–21*

Though He slay me, yet will I trust Him.
Even so, I will defend my own ways before Him.
He also shall be my salvation,
For a hypocrite could not come before Him.

*Job 13:15–16*

It is good for me that I have been afflicted,
That I may learn Your statutes.
Let, I pray, Your merciful kindness be for my comfort,
According to Your word to Your servant.

Let Your tender mercies come to me, that I may live;
For Your law is my delight.

*Psalm 119:71, 76—77*

Blessed is the man who endures temptation; for when he has
been approved, he will receive the crown of life which the Lord
has promised to those who love Him . . .
for he observes himself, goes away, and immediately forgets
what kind of man he was.

*James 1:12, 24*

Then Job arose, tore his robe, and shaved his head; and he
fell to the ground and worshiped.
And he said:
"Naked I came from my mother's womb,
And naked shall I return there.
The LORD gave, and the LORD has taken away;
Blessed be the name of the LORD."
In all this Job did not sin nor charge God with wrong.

*Job 1:20—22*

But He knows the way that I take;
When He has tested me,
I shall come forth as gold.
My foot has held fast to His steps;
I have kept His way and not turned aside.

*Job 23:10—11*

# How to Handle Suffering

Therefore, since Christ suffered for us in the flesh, arm yourselves also with the same mind, for he who has suffered in the flesh has ceased from sin,

that he no longer should live the rest of his time in the flesh for the lusts of men, but for the will of God.

Beloved, do not think it strange concerning the fiery trial which is to try you, as though some strange thing happened to you;

but rejoice to the extent that you partake of Christ's sufferings, that when His glory is revealed, you may also be glad with exceeding joy.

If you are reproached for the name of Christ, blessed are you, for the Spirit of glory and of God rests upon you. On their part He is blasphemed, but on your part He is glorified.

But let none of you suffer as a murderer, a thief, an evildoer, or as a busybody in other people's matters.

Yet if anyone suffers as a Christian, let him not be ashamed, but let him glorify God in this matter.

For the time has come for judgment to begin at the house of God; and if it begins with us first, what will be the end of those who do not obey the gospel of God?

*1 Peter 4:1–2, 12–17*

The righteous cry out, and the LORD hears,
And delivers them out of all their troubles.
The LORD is near to those who have a broken heart,
And saves such as have a contrite spirit.
Many are the afflictions of the righteous,
But the LORD delivers him out of them all.

*Psalm 34:17–19*


"For whom the LORD loves He chastens,
And scourges every son whom He receives."

If you endure chastening, God deals with you as with sons; for what son is there whom a father does not chasten?

But if you are without chastening, of which all have become partakers, then you are illegitimate and not sons.

Now no chastening seems to be joyful for the present, but painful; nevertheless, afterward it yields the peaceable fruit of righteousness to those who have been trained by it.

Therefore strengthen the hands which hang down, and the feeble knees,

and make straight paths for your feet, so that what is lame may not be dislocated, but rather be healed.

*Hebrews 12:6–8, 11–13*


We are hard-pressed on every side, yet not crushed; we are perplexed, but not in despair;

persecuted, but not forsaken; struck down, but not destroyed—

always carrying about in the body the dying of the Lord Jesus, that the life of Jesus also may be manifested in our body.

For our light affliction, which is but for a moment, is working for us a far more exceeding and eternal weight of glory,

while we do not look at the things which are seen, but at the things which are not seen. For the things which are seen are temporary, but the things which are not seen are eternal.

*2 Corinthians 4:8–10, 17–18*

But may the God of all grace, who called us to His eternal glory by Christ Jesus, after you have suffered a while, perfect, establish, strengthen, and settle you.

To Him be the glory and the dominion forever and ever. Amen.

*1 Peter 5:10–11*

For what credit is it if, when you are beaten for your faults, you take it patiently? But when you do good and suffer, if you take it patiently, this is commendable before God.

For to this you were called, because Christ also suffered for us, leaving us an example, that you should follow His steps.

*1 Peter 2:20–21*

And if children, then heirs—heirs of God and joint heirs with Christ, if indeed we suffer with Him, that we may also be glorified together.

For I consider that the sufferings of this present time are not worthy to be compared with the glory which shall be revealed in us.

*Romans 8:17–18*

You therefore must endure hardship as a good soldier of Jesus Christ.

*2 Timothy 2:3*

But we see Jesus, who was made a little lower than the angels, for the suffering of death crowned with glory and honor, that He, by the grace of God, might taste death for everyone.

For it was fitting for Him, for whom are all things and by whom are all things, in bringing many sons to glory, to make the captain of their salvation perfect through sufferings.

*Hebrews 2:9–10*

Though He was a Son, yet He learned obedience by the things which He suffered.

And having been perfected, He became the author of eternal salvation to all who obey Him.

*Hebrews 5:8–9*

Blessed is the man who endures temptation; for when he has been approved, he will receive the crown of life which the Lord has promised to those who love Him.

*James 1:12*

I know how to be abased, and I know how to abound. Everywhere and in all things I have learned both to be full and to be hungry, both to abound and to suffer need.

I can do all things through Christ who strengthens me.

*Philippians 4:12–13*

Therefore do not be ashamed of the testimony of our Lord, nor of me His prisoner, but share with me in the sufferings for the gospel according to the power of God,

For this reason I also suffer these things; nevertheless I am not ashamed, for I know whom I have believed and am persuaded that He is able to keep what I have committed to Him until that Day.

*2 Timothy 1:8, 12*

This is a faithful saying:
For if we died with Him,
We shall also live with Him.
If we endure,
We shall also reign with Him.
If we deny Him,
He also will deny us.

*2 Timothy 2:11–12*

My brethren, take the prophets, who spoke in the name of the Lord, as an example of suffering and patience.

Indeed we count them blessed who endure. You have heard of the perseverance of Job and seen the end intended by the Lord—that the Lord is very compassionate and merciful.

*James 5:10–11*

Therefore let those who suffer according to the will of God commit their souls to Him in doing good, as to a faithful Creator.

*1 Peter 4:19*

# How to Survive
# Financial Problems

For the love of money is a root of all kinds of evil, for which some have strayed from the faith in their greediness, and pierced themselves through with many sorrows.

But you, O man of God, flee these things and pursue righteousness, godliness, faith, love, patience, gentleness.

*1 Timothy 6:10–11*

Not that I speak in regard to need, for I have learned in whatever state I am, to be content:

I know how to be abased, and I know how to abound. Everywhere and in all things I have learned both to be full and to be hungry, both to abound and to suffer need.

I can do all things through Christ who strengthens me.

*Philippians 4:11–13*

Therefore do not worry, saying, "What shall we eat?" or "What shall we drink?" or "What shall we wear?"

For after all these things the Gentiles seek. For your heavenly Father knows that you need all these things.

But seek first the kingdom of God and His righteousness, and all these things shall be added to you.

Therefore do not worry about tomorrow, for tomorrow

will worry about its own things. Sufficient for the day is its own trouble.

Matthew 6:31–34

Trust in the Lord, and do good;
Dwell in the land, and feed on His faithfulness.
Delight yourself also in the Lord,
And He shall give you the desires of your heart.

Psalm 37:3–4

Command those who are rich in this present age not to be haughty, nor to trust in uncertain riches but in the living God, who gives us richly all things to enjoy.

Let them do good, that they be rich in good works, ready to give, willing to share,

storing up for themselves a good foundation for the time to come, that they may lay hold on eternal life.

1 Timothy 6:17–19

This poor man cried out, and the Lord heard him,
And saved him out of all his troubles.
The angel of the Lord encamps all around those who fear Him,
And delivers them.
Oh, taste and see that the Lord is good;
Blessed is the man who trusts in Him!
Oh, fear the Lord, you His saints!
There is no want to those who fear Him.

The young lions lack and suffer hunger;
But those who seek the LORD shall not lack any good thing.

*Psalm 34:6–10*

And the Lord said, "Who then is that faithful and wise steward, whom his master will make ruler over his household, to give them their portion of food in due season?

Blessed is that servant whom his master will find so doing when he comes.

Truly, I say to you that he will make him ruler over all that he has."

*Luke 12:42–44*

If then God so clothes the grass, which today is in the field and tomorrow is thrown into the oven, how much more will He clothe you, O you of little faith?

And do not seek what you should eat or what you should drink, nor have an anxious mind.

For all these things the nations of the world seek after, and your Father knows that you need these things.

But seek the kingdom of God, and all these things shall be added to you.

*Luke 12:28–31*

And when He had fasted forty days and forty nights, afterward He was hungry.

Now when the tempter came to Him, he said, "If You are the Son of God, command that these stones become bread."

But He answered and said, "It is written, 'Man shall not live by bread alone, but by every word that proceeds from the mouth of God.'"

*Matthew 4:2—4*

I have been young, and now am old;
Yet I have not seen the righteous forsaken,
Nor his descendants begging bread.
He is ever merciful, and lends;
And his descendants are blessed.

*Psalm 37:25—26*

They wandered in the wilderness in a desolate way;
They found no city to dwell in.
Hungry and thirsty,
Their soul fainted in them.
Then they cried out to the LORD in their trouble,
And He delivered them out of their distresses.
And He led them forth by the right way,
That they might go to a city for a dwelling place.
Oh, that men would give thanks to the LORD for His goodness,
And for His wonderful works to the children of men!

*Psalm 107:4—8*

The LORD also will be a refuge for the oppressed,
A refuge in times of trouble.

And those who know Your name will put their trust in You;
For You, LORD, have not forsaken those who seek You.

*Psalm 9:9–10*

And He said to them, "Take heed and beware of covetousness, for one's life does not consist in the abundance of the things he possesses."

*Luke 12:15*

So we may boldly say:
"The LORD is my helper;
I will not fear.
What can man do to me?"

*Hebrews 13:6*

Then He said to His disciples, "Therefore I say to you, do not worry about your life, what you will eat; nor about the body, what you will put on.

Life is more than food, and the body is more than clothing.

Consider the ravens, for they neither sow nor reap, which have neither storehouse nor barn; and God feeds them. Of how much more value are you than the birds?"

*Luke 12:22–24*

And my God shall supply all your need according to His riches in glory by Christ Jesus.

*Philippians 4:19*

For you have need of endurance, so that after you have done the will of God, you may receive the promise.

*Hebrews 10:36*


He who trusts in his riches will fall,
But the righteous will flourish like foliage.

*Proverbs 11:28*


There is one who makes himself rich, yet has nothing;
And one who makes himself poor, yet has great riches.
Wealth gained by dishonesty will be diminished,
But he who gathers by labor will increase.

*Proverbs 13:7, 11*


Remove falsehood and lies far from me;
Give me neither poverty nor riches—
Feed me with the food allotted to me.

*Proverbs 30:8*


Listen, my beloved brethren: Has God not chosen the poor of this world to be rich in faith and heirs of the kingdom which He promised to those who love Him?

*James 2:5*

# How to Handle Stress

Peace I leave with you, My peace I give to you; not as the world gives do I give to you. Let not your heart be troubled, neither let it be afraid.

*John 14:27*

Be anxious for nothing, but in everything by prayer and supplication, with thanksgiving, let your requests be made known to God;

and the peace of God, which surpasses all understanding, will guard your hearts and minds through Christ Jesus.

Finally, brethren, whatever things are true, whatever things are noble, whatever things are just, whatever things are pure, whatever things are lovely, whatever things are of good report, if there is any virtue and if there is anything praiseworthy—meditate on these things.

*Philippians 4:6–8*

Fear not, for I am with you;
Be not dismayed, for I am your God.
I will strengthen you,
Yes, I will help you,
I will uphold you with My righteous right hand.

*Isaiah 41:10*

He makes me to lie down in green pastures;
He leads me beside the still waters.
He restores my soul;
He leads me in the paths of righteousness
For His name's sake.
Yea, though I walk through the valley of the shadow of death,
I will fear no evil;
For You are with me;
Your rod and Your staff, they comfort me.

*Psalm 23:2–4*

Casting all your care upon Him, for He cares for you.

Be sober, be vigilant; because your adversary the devil walks about like a roaring lion, seeking whom he may devour.

Resist him, steadfast in the faith, knowing that the same sufferings are experienced by your brotherhood in the world.

But may the God of all grace, who called us to His eternal glory by Christ Jesus, after you have suffered a while, perfect, establish, strengthen, and settle you.

To Him be the glory and the dominion forever and ever. Amen.

*1 Peter 5:7–11*

He will not be afraid of evil tidings;
His heart is steadfast, trusting in the LORD.
His heart is established;

He will not be afraid,
Until he sees his desire upon his enemies.

*Psalm 112:7–8*

God is our refuge and strength,
A very present help in trouble.
Therefore we will not fear,
Even though the earth be removed,
And though the mountains be carried into the midst of
the sea;
Though its waters roar and be troubled,
Though the mountains shake with its swelling. Selah

*Psalm 46:1–3*

Whenever I am afraid,
I will trust in You.
In God (I will praise His word),
In God I have put my trust;
I will not fear.
What can flesh do to me?
You number my wanderings;
Put my tears into Your bottle;
Are they not in Your book?
When I cry out to You,
Then my enemies will turn back;
This I know, because God is for me.

*Psalm 56:3–4, 8–9*

Surely He shall deliver you from the snare of the fowler
And from the perilous pestilence.
He shall cover you with His feathers,
And under His wings you shall take refuge;
His truth shall be your shield and buckler.
You shall not be afraid of the terror by night,
Nor of the arrow that flies by day,
Nor of the pestilence that walks in darkness,
Nor of the destruction that lays waste at noonday.
A thousand may fall at your side,
And ten thousand at your right hand;
But it shall not come near you.

*Psalm 91:3–7*


Hungry and thirsty,
Their soul fainted in them.
Then they cried out to the LORD in their trouble,
And He delivered them out of their distresses.
And He led them forth by the right way,
That they might go to a city for a dwelling place.

*Psalm 107:5–7*


The LORD shall preserve you from all evil;
He shall preserve your soul.
The LORD shall preserve your going out and your coming in
From this time forth, and even forevermore.

*Psalm 121:7–8*

But He was in the stern, asleep on a pillow. And they awoke Him and said to Him, "Teacher, do you not care that we are perishing?"

Then He arose and rebuked the wind, and said to the sea, "Peace, be still!" And the wind ceased and there was a great calm.

But He said to them, "Why are you so fearful? How is it that you have no faith?"

*Mark 4:38–40*


Be angry, and do not sin: do not let the sun go down on your wrath,
nor give place to the devil.

*Ephesians 4:26–27*


But You, O LORD, are a shield for me,
My glory and the One who lifts up my head.
I cried to the LORD with my voice,
And He heard me from His holy hill. Selah
I will not be afraid of ten thousands of people
Who have set themselves against me all around.

*Psalm 3:3–4, 6*


Therefore do not worry, saying, "What shall we eat?" or "What shall we drink?" or "What shall we wear?"

For after all these things the Gentiles seek. For your heavenly Father knows that you need all these things.

But seek first the kingdom of God and His righteousness, and all these things shall be added to you.

Therefore do not worry about tomorrow, for tomorrow will worry about its own things. Sufficient for the day is its own trouble.

*Matthew 6:31–34*

You will keep him in perfect peace,
Whose mind is stayed on You,
Because he trusts in You.
Trust in the LORD forever,
For in YAH, the LORD, is everlasting strength.

*Isaiah 26:3–4*

For God has not given us a spirit of fear, but of power and of love and of a sound mind . . .

who has saved us and called us with a holy calling, not according to our works, but according to His own purpose and grace which was given to us in Christ Jesus before time began.

*2 Timothy 1:7, 9*

Come to Me, all you who labor and are heavy laden, and I will give you rest.

Take My yoke upon you and learn from Me, for I am gentle and lowly in heart, and you will find rest for your souls.

For My yoke is easy and My burden is light.

*Matthew 11:28–30*

# HOW TO OVERCOME DESPAIR

We are hard-pressed on every side, yet not crushed; we are perplexed, but not in despair;

persecuted, but not forsaken; struck down, but not destroyed—

Therefore we do not lose heart. Even though our outward man is perishing, yet the inward man is being renewed day by day.

For our light affliction, which is but for a moment, is working for us a far more exceeding and eternal weight of glory,

while we do not look at the things which are seen, but at the things which are not seen. For the things which are seen are temporary, but the things which are not seen are eternal.

*2 Corinthians 4:8–9, 16–18*

For if you return to the LORD, your brethren and your children will be treated with compassion by those who lead them captive, so that they may come back to this land; for the LORD your God is gracious and merciful, and will not turn His face from you if you return to Him.

*2 Chronicles 30:9*

Let your conduct be without covetousness; be content with such things as you have. For He Himself has said, "I will never leave you nor forsake you."

So we may boldly say:

"The LORD is my helper;
I will not fear.
What can man do to me?"

*Hebrews 13:5–6*

Come to Me, all you who labor and are heavy laden, and I will give you rest.

Take My yoke upon you and learn from Me, for I am gentle and lowly in heart, and you will find rest for your souls.

For My yoke is easy and My burden is light.

*Matthew 11:28–30*

For His anger is but for a moment,
His favor is for life;
Weeping may endure for a night,
But joy comes in the morning.
I cried out to You, O LORD;
And to the LORD made supplication:
"What profit is there in my blood,
When I go down to the pit?
Will the dust praise You?
Will it declare Your truth?
Hear, O LORD, and have mercy on me;
LORD, be my helper!"
You have turned for me my mourning into dancing;

You have put off my sackcloth and clothed me with gladness,

To the end that my glory may sing praise to You and not be silent.

O Lord my God, I will give thanks to You forever.

*Psalm 30:5, 8—12*

Finally, brethren, whatever things are true, whatever things are noble, whatever things are just, whatever things are pure, whatever things are lovely, whatever things are of good report, if there is any virtue and if there is anything praiseworthy—meditate on these things.

*Philippians 4:8*

He has not dealt with us according to our sins,
Nor punished us according to our iniquities.
For as the heavens are high above the earth,
So great is His mercy toward those who fear Him;
As far as the east is from the west,
So far has He removed our transgressions from us.

*Psalm 103:10—12*

This hope we have as an anchor of the soul, both sure and steadfast, and which enters the Presence behind the veil.

*Hebrews 6:19*

And so, after he had patiently endured, he obtained the promise.

*Hebrews 6:15*

And let us not grow weary while doing good, for in due season we shall reap if we do not lose heart.

*Galatians 6:9*

The Spirit of the Lord GOD is upon Me,
Because the LORD has anointed Me
To preach good tidings to the poor;
He has sent Me to heal the brokenhearted,
To proclaim liberty to the captives,
And the opening of the prison to those who are bound;
To proclaim the acceptable year of the LORD,
And the day of vengeance of our God;
To comfort all who mourn,
To console those who mourn in Zion,
To give them beauty for ashes,
The oil of joy for mourning,
The garment of praise for the spirit of heaviness;
That they may be called trees of righteousness,
The planting of the LORD, that He may be glorified.

*Isaiah 61:1–3*

He gives power to the weak,
And to those who have no might He increases strength.
Even the youths shall faint and be weary,
And the young men shall utterly fall,
But those who wait on the LORD
Shall renew their strength;
They shall mount up with wings like eagles,

They shall run and not be weary,
They shall walk and not faint.

*Isaiah 40:29–31*

He heals the brokenhearted
And binds up their wounds.

*Psalm 147:3*

# How to Maintain Hope

Through the LORD's mercies we are not consumed,
Because His compassions fail not.
They are new every morning;
Great is your faithfulness.
"The LORD is my portion," says my soul,
"Therefore I hope in Him!"

*Lamentations 3:22—24*

Therefore, having been justified by faith, we have peace with God through our Lord Jesus Christ,

through whom also we have access by faith into this grace in which we stand, and rejoice in hope of the glory of God.

And not only that, but we also glory in tribulations, knowing that tribulation produces perseverance;

and perseverance, character; and character, hope.

Now hope does not disappoint, because the love of God has been poured out in our hearts by the Holy Spirit who was given to us.

*Romans 5:1—5*

Now may the God of hope fill you with all joy and peace in believing, that you may abound in hope by the power of the Holy Spirit.

*Romans 15:13*

But let us who are of the day be sober, putting on the breastplate of faith and love, and as a helmet the hope of salvation.

For God did not appoint us to wrath, but to obtain salvation through our Lord Jesus Christ.

*1 Thessalonians 5:8–9*

Therefore do not worry about tomorrow, for tomorrow will worry about its own things. Sufficient for the day is its own trouble.

*Matthew 6:34*

Let your conduct be without covetousness; be content with such things as you have. For He Himself has said, "I will never leave you nor forsake you."

So we may boldly say:

"The LORD is my helper;

I will not fear.

What can man do to me?"

*Hebrews 13:5–6*

Behold, the eye of the LORD is on those who fear Him,

On those who hope in His mercy,

To deliver their soul from death,

And to keep them alive in famine.
Our soul waits for the LORD;
He is our help and our shield.
For our heart shall rejoice in Him,
Because we have trusted in His holy name.
Let Your mercy, O LORD, be upon us,
Just as we hope in you.

*Psalm 33:18—22*


Cast your burden on the LORD,
And He shall sustain you;
He shall never permit the righteous to be moved.

*Psalm 55:22*


My soul, wait silently for God alone,
For my expectation is from Him.
He only is my rock and my salvation;
He is my defense;
I shall not be moved.
In God is my salvation and my glory;
The rock of my strength,
And my refuge, is in God.

*Psalm 62:5—7*


I would have lost heart, unless I had believed
That I would see the goodness of the LORD
In the land of the living.
Wait on the LORD;
Be of good courage,

And He shall strengthen your heart;
Wait, I say, on the LORD!

*Psalm 27:13–14*


You are my hiding place and my shield;
I hope in Your word.

*Psalm 119:114*


But those who wait on the LORD
Shall renew their strength;
They shall mount up with wings like eagles,
They shall run and not be weary,
They shall walk and not faint.

*Isaiah 40:31*


And so, after he had patiently endured, he obtained the promise . . .

that by two immutable things, in which it is impossible for God to lie, we might have strong consolation, who have fled for refuge to lay hold of the hope set before us.

This hope we have as an anchor of the soul, both sure and steadfast, and which enters the Presence behind the veil.

*Hebrews 6:15, 18–19*


Finally, brethren, whatever things are true, whatever things are noble, whatever things are just, whatever things are pure, whatever things are lovely, whatever things are of good report, if there is any virtue and if there is anything praiseworthy—meditate on these things.

I can do all things through Christ who strengthens me.

*Philippians 4:8, 13*

Or does He say it altogether for our sakes? For our sakes, no doubt, this is written, that he who plows should plow in hope, and he who threshes in hope should be partaker of his hope.

*1 Corinthians 9:10*

But if we hope for what we do not see, we eagerly wait for it with perseverance.

What then shall we say to these things? If God is for us, who can be against us?

Yet in all these things we are more than conquerors through Him who loved us.

For I am persuaded that neither death nor life, nor angels nor principalities nor powers, nor things present nor things to come,

nor height nor depth, nor any other created thing, shall be able to separate us from the love of God which is in Christ Jesus our Lord.

*Romans 8:25, 31, 37–39*

Do not be a terror to me;
You are my hope in the day of doom.

*Jeremiah 17:17*

# How to Enter into His Rest

Commit your way to the LORD,
Trust also in Him,
And He shall bring it to pass.
He shall bring forth your righteousness as the light,
And your justice as the noonday.
Rest in the LORD, and wait patiently for Him;
Do not fret because of him who prospers in his way,
Because of the man who brings wicked schemes to pass.

*Psalm 37:5–7*

Finally, brethren, whatever things are true, whatever things are noble, whatever things are just, whatever things are pure, whatever things are lovely, whatever things are of good report, if there is any virtue and if there is anything praiseworthy—meditate on these things.

Not that I speak in regard to need, for I have learned in whatever state I am, to be content:

I know how to be abased, and I know how to abound. Everywhere and in all things I have learned both to be full and to be hungry, both to abound and to suffer need.

I can do all things through Christ who strengthens me.

And my God shall supply all your need according to His riches in glory by Christ Jesus.

*Philippians 4:8, 11–13, 19*

Come to Me, all you who labor and are heavy laden, and I will give you rest.

Take My yoke upon you and learn from Me, for I am gentle and lowly in heart, and you will find rest for your souls.

For My yoke is easy and My burden is light.

*Matthew 11:28–30*

There remains therefore a rest for the people of God.

Let us therefore be diligent to enter that rest, lest anyone fall according to the same example of disobedience.

Seeing then that we have a great High Priest who has passed through the heavens, Jesus the Son of God, let us hold fast our confession.

*Hebrews 4:9, 11, 14*

For thus says the Lord GOD, the Holy One of Israel:

"In returning and rest you shall be saved;

In quietness and confidence shall be your strength."

But you would not,

Therefore the LORD will wait, that He may be gracious to you;

And therefore He will be exalted, that He may have mercy on you. For the LORD is a God of justice;

Blessed are all those who wait for Him.

*Isaiah 30:15, 18*

The LORD is your keeper;
The LORD is your shade at your right hand.
The sun shall not strike you by day,
Nor the moon by night.
The LORD shall preserve you from all evil;
He shall preserve your soul.
The LORD shall preserve your going out and your coming in
From this time forth, and even forevermore.

*Psalm 121:5–8*

Cast your burden on the LORD,
And He shall sustain you;
He shall never permit the righteous to be moved.

*Psalm 55:22*

And He said, "My Presence will go with you, and I will give you rest."

*Exodus 33:14*

And we know that all things work together for good to those who love God, to those who are the called according to His purpose.

*Romans 8:28*

Therefore, having been justified by faith, we have peace with God through our Lord Jesus Christ,
through whom also we have access by faith into this grace in which we stand, and rejoice in hope of the glory of God.

*Romans 5:1–2*

For God is not the author of confusion but of peace, as in all the churches of the saints.

*1 Corinthians 14:33*

The fear of man brings a snare,
But whoever trusts in the LORD shall be safe.

*Proverbs 29:25*

But seek first the kingdom of God and His righteousness, and all these things shall be added to you.

Therefore do not worry about tomorrow, for tomorrow will worry about its own things. Sufficient for the day is its own trouble.

*Matthew 6:33–34*

Furthermore, we have had human fathers who corrected us, and we paid them respect. Shall we not much more readily be in subjection to the Father of spirits and live?

*Hebrews 12:9*

Therefore submit to God. Resist the devil and he will flee from you.

*James 4:7*

But the Lord is faithful, who will establish you and guard you from the evil one.

*2 Thessalonians 3:3*

# How to Be Established in Trust

Blessed is the man who trusts in the LORD,
And whose hope is the LORD.
For he shall be like a tree planted by the waters,
Which spreads out its roots by the river,
And will not fear when heat comes;
But its leaf will be green,
And will not be anxious in the year of drought,
Nor will cease from yielding fruit.

*Jeremiah 17:7–8*

And we know that all things work together for good to those who love God, to those who are the called according to His purpose.

*Romans 8:28*

I will say of the LORD, "He is my refuge and my fortress;
My God, in Him I will trust."
Surely He shall deliver you from the snare of the fowler
And from the perilous pestilence.
He shall cover you with His feathers,
And under His wings you shall take refuge;
His truth shall be your shield and buckler.

*Psalm 91:2–4*

Casting all your care upon Him, for He cares for you.

*1 Peter 5:7*

But the salvation of the righteous is from the LORD;
He is their strength in the time of trouble.
And the LORD shall help them and deliver them;
He shall deliver them from the wicked,
And save them,
Because they trust in Him.

*Psalm 37:39–40*

He will not be afraid of evil tidings;
His heart is steadfast, trusting in the LORD.
His heart is established;
He will not be afraid,
Until he sees his desire upon his enemies.

*Psalm 112:7–8*

Yes, we had the sentence of death in ourselves, that we should not trust in ourselves but in God who raises the dead, who delivered us from so great a death, and does deliver us; in whom we trust that He will still deliver us.

*2 Corinthians 1:9–10*

Therefore we will not fear,
Even though the earth be removed,
And though the mountains be carried into the midst of the sea.

*Psalm 46:2*

Through God we will do valiantly,
For it is He who shall tread down our enemies.

*Psalm 60:12*


Whenever I am afraid,
I will trust in You.
In God (I will praise His word),
In God I have put my trust;
I will not fear.
What can flesh do to me?
In God I have put my trust;
I will not be afraid.
What can man do to me?
For You have delivered my soul from death.
Have You not kept my feet from falling,
That I may walk before God
In the light of the living?

*Psalm 56:3–4, 11, 13*


The LORD is on my side;
I will not fear.
What can man do to me?
It is better to trust in the LORD
Than to put confidence in man.

*Psalm 118:6, 8*


He will not allow your foot to be moved;
He who keeps you will not slumber.

*Psalm 121:3*

Those who trust in the LORD
Are like Mount Zion,
Which cannot be moved, but abides forever.
Do good, O LORD, to those who are good,
And to those who are upright in their hearts.

*Psalm 125:1, 4*


He who heeds the word wisely will find good,
And whoever trusts in the LORD, happy is he.

*Proverbs 16:20*


Every word of God is pure;
He is a shield to those who put their trust in Him.

*Proverbs 30:5*


But You, O LORD, are a shield for me,
My glory and the One who lifts up my head.
I cried to the LORD with my voice,
And He heard me from His holy hill. Selah
I lay down and slept;
I awoke, for the LORD sustained me.
I will not be afraid of ten thousands of people
Who have set themselves against me all around.

*Psalm 3:3–6*


The LORD redeems the soul of His servants,
And none of those who trust in Him shall be condemned.

*Psalm 34:22*

Uphold my steps in Your paths,
That my footsteps may not slip.
I have called upon You, for You will hear me, O God;
Incline Your ear to me, and hear my speech.
Show your marvelous lovingkindness by Your right hand,
O You who save those who trust in You
From those who rise up against them.
Keep me as the apple of Your eye;
Hide me under the shadow of Your wings.

*Psalm 17:5—8*

# HOW TO HAVE GOD'S DIVINE PROTECTION

He who dwells in the secret place of the Most High
Shall abide under the shadow of the Almighty.
I will say of the LORD, "He is my refuge and my fortress;
My God, in Him I will trust."
Surely He shall deliver you from the snare of the fowler
And from the perilous pestilence.
He shall cover you with His feathers,
And under His wings you shall take refuge;
His truth shall be your shield and buckler.
You shall not be afraid of the terror by night,
Nor of the arrow that flies by day,
Nor of the pestilence that walks in darkness,
Nor of the destruction that lays waste at noonday.
A thousand may fall at your side,
And ten thousand at your right hand;
But it shall not come near you.
Only with your eyes shall you look,
And see the reward of the wicked.
Because you have made the LORD, who is my refuge,
Even the Most High, your dwelling place,
No evil shall befall you,

Nor shall any plague come near your dwelling;
For He shall give His angels charge over you,
To keep you in all your ways.
In their hands they shall bear you up,
Lest you dash your foot against a stone.
You shall tread upon the lion and the cobra,
The young lion and the serpent you shall trample under-
foot.
"Because he has set his love upon Me, therefore I will
deliver him;
I will set him on high, because he has known My name.
He shall call upon Me, and I will answer him;
I will be with him in trouble;
I will deliver him and honor him.
With long life I will satisfy him,
And show him My salvation."

*Psalm 91:1–16*


The LORD is my light and my salvation;
Whom shall I fear?
The LORD is the strength of my life;
Of whom shall I be afraid?
For in the time of trouble
He shall hide me in His pavilion;
In the secret place of His tabernacle
He shall hide me;
He shall set me high upon a rock.

*Psalm 27:1, 5*

When you pass through the waters, I will be with you;
And through the rivers, they shall not overflow you.
When you walk through the fire, you shall not be burned,
Nor shall the flame scorch you.

*Isaiah 43:2*

But let all those rejoice who put their trust in You;
Let them ever shout for joy, because You defend them;
Let those also who love Your name
Be joyful in You.
For You, O LORD, will bless the righteous;
With favor You will surround him as with a shield.

*Psalm 5:11–12*

The beloved of the LORD shall dwell in safety by Him,
Who shelters him all the day long;
And he shall dwell between His shoulders.
The eternal God is your refuge,
And underneath are the everlasting arms;
He will thrust out the enemy from before you,
And will say, "Destroy!"

*Deuteronomy 33:12, 27*

Be anxious for nothing, but in everything by prayer and
supplication, with thanksgiving, let your requests be made
known to God;

and the peace of God, which surpasses all understanding, will guard your hearts and minds through Christ Jesus.

*Philippians 4:6–7*

The angel of the LORD encamps all around those who fear Him,
And delivers them.

*Psalm 34:7*

Are not two sparrows sold for a copper coin? And not one of them falls to the ground apart from your Father's will.
But the very hairs of your head are all numbered.
Do not fear therefore; you are of more value than many sparrows.

*Matthew 10:29–31*

The fear of man brings a snare,
But whoever trusts in the LORD shall be safe.

*Proverbs 29:25*

Yea, though I walk through the valley of the shadow of death,
I will fear no evil;
For You are with me;
Your rod and Your staff, they comfort me.

*Psalm 23:4*

So shall they fear
The name of the LORD from the west,
And His glory from the rising of the sun;
When the enemy comes in like a flood,
The Spirit of the LORD will lift up a standard against him.

*Isaiah 59:19*

I will both lie down in peace, and sleep;
For You alone, O LORD, make me dwell in safety.

*Psalm 4:8*

# HOW TO FIND CONTENTMENT

Therefore do not worry, saying, "What shall we eat?" or "What shall we drink?" or "What shall we wear?"

For after all these things the Gentiles seek. For your heavenly Father knows that you need all these things.

But seek first the kingdom of God and His righteousness, and all these things shall be added to you.

Therefore do not worry about tomorrow, for tomorrow will worry about its own things. Sufficient for the day is its own trouble.

*Matthew 6:31–34*

You will keep him in perfect peace,
Whose mind is stayed on You,
Trust in the LORD forever,
For in YAH, the LORD, is everlasting strength.

*Isaiah 26:3–4*

Let your conduct be without covetousness; be content with such things as you have. For He Himself has said, "I will never leave you nor forsake you."

So we may boldly say:
"The LORD is my helper;
I will not fear.

What can man do to me?"

*Hebrews 13:5–6*

Be anxious for nothing, but in everything by prayer and supplication, with thanksgiving, let your requests be made known to God;

and the peace of God, which surpasses all understanding, will guard your hearts and minds through Christ Jesus.

Not that I speak in regard to need, for I have learned in whatever state I am, to be content:

I know how to be abased, and I know how to abound. Everywhere and in all things I have learned both to be full and to be hungry, both to abound and to suffer need.

I can do all things through Christ who strengthens me.

*Philippians 4:6–7, 11–13*

And we know that all things work together for good to those who love God, to those who are the called according to His purpose.

*Romans 8:28*

"For the mountains shall depart
And the hills be removed,
But My kindness shall not depart from you,
Nor shall My covenant of peace be removed,"
says the LORD, who has mercy on you.
"All your children shall be taught by the LORD,
And great shall be the peace of your children.
No weapon formed against you shall prosper,

And every tongue which rises against you in judgment
You shall condemn.
This is the heritage of the servants of the LORD,
And their righteousness is from Me,"
says the LORD.

*Isaiah 54:10, 13, 17*

There is therefore now no condemnation to those who are in Christ Jesus, who do not walk according to the flesh, but according to the Spirit.

For the law of the Spirit of life in Christ Jesus has made me free from the law of sin and death.

For those who live according to the flesh set their minds on the things of the flesh, but those who live according to the Spirit, the things of the Spirit.

For to be carnally minded is death, but to be spiritually minded is life and peace.

*Romans 8:1–2, 5–6*

The Spirit Himself bears witness with our spirit that we are children of God,

and if children, then heirs—heirs of God and joint heirs with Christ, if indeed we suffer with Him, that we may also be glorified together.

For I consider that the sufferings of this present time are not worthy to be compared with the glory which shall be revealed in us.

*Romans 8:16–18*

He who dwells in the secret place of the Most High
Shall abide under the shadow of the Almighty.
I will say of the LORD, "He is my refuge and my fortress;
My God, in Him I will trust."

*Psalm 91:1–2*


The LORD upholds all who fall,
And raises up all who are bowed down.
The eyes of all look expectantly to You,
And You give them their food in due season.
You open Your hand
And satisfy the desire of every living thing.

*Psalm 145:14–16*


But I discipline my body and bring it into subjection, lest, when I have preached to others, I myself should become disqualified.

*1 Corinthians 9:27*


Now godliness with contentment is great gain.

For we brought nothing into this world, and it is certain we can carry nothing out.

And having food and clothing, with these we shall be content.

*1 Timothy 6:6–8*


But You, O LORD, are a shield for me,
My glory and the One who lifts up my head.
I cried to the LORD with my voice,

And He heard me from His holy hill. Selah
I lay down and slept;
I awoke, for the LORD sustained me.
I will not be afraid of ten thousands of people
Who have set themselves against me all around.

*Psalm 3:3–6*


For we who have believed do enter that rest, as He has said:
"So I swore in My wrath,
'They shall not enter My rest,'"
although the works were finished from the foundation of
the world.

*Hebrews 4:3*


And be found in Him, not having my own righteousness,
which is from the law, but that which is through faith in
Christ, the righteousness which is from God by faith.

*Philippians 3:9*


The LORD is my shepherd; I shall not want.

*Psalm 23:1*


The LORD will guide you continually,
And satisfy your soul in drought,
And strengthen your bones;
You shall be like a watered garden,
And like a spring of water, whose waters do not fail.

*Isaiah 58:11*

I will lift up my eyes to the hills—
From whence comes my help?
My help comes from the LORD,
Who made heaven and earth.
He will not allow your foot to be moved;
He who keeps you will not slumber.
The LORD is your keeper;
The LORD is your shade at your right hand.
The LORD shall preserve your going out and your coming in
From this time forth, and even forevermore.

*Psalm 121:1–3, 5, 8*

Shall not the Judge of all the earth do right?

*Genesis 18:25b*

Not that we are sufficient of ourselves to think of anything
as being from ourselves, but our sufficiency is from God.

*2 Corinthians 3:5*

# MINISTERING
## IN CHRIST

# What Is the Way to True Service?

When He had called the people to Himself, with His disciples also, He said to them, "Whoever desires to come after Me, let him deny himself, and take up his cross, and follow Me.

For whoever desires to save his life will lose it, but whoever loses his life for My sake and the gospel's will save it.

For what will it profit a man if he gains the whole world, and loses his own soul?

Or what will a man give in exchange for his soul?"

*Mark 8:34–37*

Abide in Me, and I in you. As the branch cannot bear fruit of itself, unless it abides in the vine, neither can you, unless you abide in Me.

I am the vine, you are the branches. He who abides in Me, and I in him, bears much fruit; for without Me you can do nothing.

*John 15:4–5*

For we do not preach ourselves, but Christ Jesus the Lord, and ourselves your bondservants for Jesus' sake.

For it is the God who commanded light to shine out of darkness, who has shone in our hearts to give the light of the knowledge of the glory of God in the face of Jesus Christ.

But we have this treasure in earthen vessels, that the excellence of the power may be of God and not of us.

*2 Corinthians 4:5–7*

And whatever you do, do it heartily, as to the Lord and not to men,

knowing that from the Lord you will receive the reward of the inheritance; for you serve the Lord Christ.

But he who does wrong will be repaid for what he has done, and there is no partiality.

*Colossians 3:23–25*

Command those who are rich in this present age not to be haughty, nor to trust in uncertain riches but in the living God, who gives us richly all things to enjoy.

Let them do good, that they be rich in good works, ready to give, willing to share,

storing up for themselves a good foundation for the time to come, that they may lay hold on eternal life.

*1 Timothy 6:17–19*

He who is faithful in what is least is faithful also in much; and he who is unjust in what is least is unjust also in much.

Therefore if you have not been faithful in the unrighteous mammon, who will commit to your trust the true riches?

And if you have not been faithful in what is another man's, who will give you what is your own?

"No servant can serve two masters; for either he will hate

the one and love the other, or else he will be loyal to the one and despise the other. You cannot serve God and mammon."

*Luke 16:10–13*

As each one has received a gift, minister it to one another, as good stewards of the manifold grace of God.

If anyone speaks, let him speak as the oracles of God. If anyone ministers, let him do it as with the ability which God supplies, that in all things God may be glorified through Jesus Christ, to whom belong the glory and the dominion forever and ever. Amen.

*1 Peter 4:10–11*

Let each one remain in the same calling in which he was called.

*1 Corinthians 7:20*

John answered and said, "A man can receive nothing unless it has been given to him from heaven."

*John 3:27*

But let each one examine his own work, and then he will have rejoicing in himself alone, and not in another.

For each one shall bear his own load.

Let him who is taught the word share in all good things with him who teaches.

And let us not grow weary while doing good, for in due season we shall reap if we do not lose heart.

*Galatians 6:4–6, 9*

Now he who plants and he who waters are one, and each one will receive his own reward according to his own labor.

For we are God's fellow workers; you are God's field, you are God's building.

*1 Corinthians 3:8—9*

For you see your calling, brethren, that not many wise according to the flesh, not many mighty, not many noble, are called.

But God has chosen the foolish things of the world to put to shame the wise, and God has chosen the weak things of the world to put to shame the things which are mighty;

and the base things of the world and the things which are despised God has chosen, and the things which are not, to bring to nothing the things that are,

that no flesh should glory in His presence.

*1 Corinthians 1:26—29*

But a certain Samaritan, as he journeyed, came where he was. And when he saw him, he had compassion.

So he went to him and bandaged his wounds, pouring on oil and wine; and he set him on his own animal, brought him to an inn, and took care of him.

*Luke 10:33—34*

In the morning sow your seed,
And in the evening do not withhold your hand;
For you do not know which will prosper,

Either this or that,
Or whether both alike will be good.

*Ecclesiastes 11:6*

And another also said, "Lord, I will follow You, but let me first go and bid them farewell who are at my house."

But Jesus said to him, "No one, having put his hand to the plow, and looking back, is fit for the kingdom of God."

*Luke 9:61–62*

So the people asked him, saying, "What shall we do then?"

He answered and said to them, "He who has two tunics, let him give to him who has none; and he who has food, let him do likewise."

*Luke 3:10–11*

By this all will know that you are My disciples, if you have love for one another.

*John 13:35*

That you may become blameless and harmless, children of God without fault in the midst of a crooked and perverse generation, among whom you shine as lights in the world,

holding fast the word of life, so that I may rejoice in the day of Christ that I have not run in vain or labored in vain.

*Philippians 2:15–16*

You did not choose Me, but I chose you and appointed you that you should go and bear fruit, and that your fruit should remain, that whatever you ask the Father in My name He may give you.

These things I command you, that you love one another.

*John 15:16–17*

And whoever does not bear his cross and come after Me cannot be My disciple.

For which of you, intending to build a tower, does not sit down first and count the cost, whether he has enough to finish it—

lest, after he has laid the foundation, and is not able to finish, all who see it begin to mock him,

saying, "This man began to build and was not able to finish."

So likewise, whoever of you does not forsake all that he has cannot be My disciple.

*Luke 14:27–30, 33*

He who calls you is faithful, who also will do it.

*I Thessalonians 5:24*

# How to Have
# an Effective Prayer Life

Be anxious for nothing, but in everything by prayer and supplication, with thanksgiving, let your requests be made known to God;

and the peace of God, which surpasses all understanding, will guard your hearts and minds through Christ Jesus.

*Philippians 4:6–7*

Assuredly, I say to you, whatever you bind on earth will be bound in heaven, and whatever you loose on earth will be loosed in heaven.

Again I say to you that if two of you agree on earth concerning anything that they ask, it will be done for them by My Father in heaven.

*Matthew 18:18–19*

Let us therefore come boldly to the throne of grace, that we may obtain mercy and find grace to help in time of need.

*Hebrews 4:16*

But without faith it is impossible to please Him, for he who comes to God must believe that He is, and that He is a rewarder of those who diligently seek Him.

*Hebrews 11:6*

Confess your trespasses to one another, and pray for one another, that you may be healed. The effective, fervent prayer of a righteous man avails much.

Elijah was a man with a nature like ours, and he prayed earnestly that it would not rain; and it did not rain on the land for three years and six months.

And he prayed again, and the heaven gave rain, and the earth produced its fruit.

*James 5:16–18*

Therefore take up the whole armor of God, that you may be able to withstand in the evil day, and having done all, to stand.

Stand therefore, having girded your waist with truth, having put on the breastplate of righteousness,

and having shod your feet with the preparation of the gospel of peace;

above all, taking the shield of faith with which you will be able to quench all the fiery darts of the wicked one.

And take the helmet of salvation, and the sword of the Spirit, which is the word of God;

praying always with all prayer and supplication in the Spirit, being watchful to this end with all perseverance and supplication for all the saints.

*Ephesians 6:13–18*

So I say to you, ask, and it will be given to you; seek, and you will find; knock, and it will be opened to you.

*Luke 11:9*

And when you pray, you shall not be like the hypocrites. For they love to pray standing in the synagogues and on the corners of the streets, that they may be seen by men. Assuredly, I say to you, they have their reward.

But you, when you pray, go into your room, and when you have shut your door, pray to your Father who is in the secret place; and your Father who sees in secret will reward you openly.

*Matthew 6:5–6*

Then He spoke a parable to them, that men always ought to pray and not lose heart.

*Luke 18:1*

For the eyes of the LORD are on the righteous,
And His ears are open to their prayers;
But the face of the LORD is against those who do evil.

*1 Peter 3:12*

Evening and morning and at noon
I will pray, and cry aloud,
And He shall hear my voice.

*Psalm 55:17*

Let us come before His presence with thanksgiving;
Let us shout joyfully to Him with psalms.

*Psalm 95:2*

I cry out to the LORD with my voice;
With my voice to the LORD I make my supplication.
I pour out my complaint before Him;
I declare before Him my trouble.

*Psalm 142:1–2*

Now this is the confidence that we have in Him, that if we ask anything according to His will, He hears us.

And if we know that He hears us, whatever we ask, we know that we have the petitions that we have asked of Him.

*1 John 5:14–15*

You will make your prayer to Him,
He will hear you,
And you will pay your vows.
You will also declare a thing,
And it will be established for you;
So light will shine on your ways.

*Job 22:27–28*

Likewise the Spirit also helps in our weaknesses. For we do not know what we should pray for as we ought, but the Spirit Himself makes intercession for us with groanings which cannot be uttered.

*Romans 8:26*

My voice You shall hear in the morning, O LORD;
In the morning I will direct it to You,
And I will look up.

*Psalm 5:3*

But know that the LORD has set apart for Himself him
who is godly;
The LORD will hear when I call to Him.

*Psalm 4:3*

Give ear, O LORD, to my prayer;
And attend to the voice of my supplications.
In the day of my trouble I will call upon You,
For You will answer me.

*Psalm 86:6–7*

But let him ask in faith, with no doubting, for he who
doubts is like a wave of the sea driven and tossed by the wind.

*James 1:6*

You called in trouble, and I delivered you;
I answered you in the secret place of thunder;
I tested you at the waters of Meribah. Selah

*Psalm 81:7*

Rejoicing in hope, patient in tribulation, continuing
steadfastly in prayer.

*Romans 12:12*

Now in the morning, having risen a long while before daylight, He went out and departed to a solitary place; and there He prayed.

*Mark 1:35*


Now it came to pass in those days that He went out to the mountain to pray, and continued all night in prayer to God.

*Luke 6:12*


LORD, I cry out to You;
Make haste to me!
Give ear to my voice when I cry out to You.
Let my prayer be set before You as incense,
The lifting up of my hands as the evening sacrifice.

*Psalm 141:1–2*


So shall My word be that goes forth from My mouth;
It shall not return to Me void,
But it shall accomplish what I please,
And it shall prosper in the thing for which I sent it.

*Isaiah 55:11*

# How to Be an Effective Witness

You are the light of the world. A city that is set on a hill cannot be hidden.

Nor do they light a lamp and put it under a basket, but on a lampstand, and it gives light to all who are in the house.

Let your light so shine before men, that they may see your good works and glorify your Father in heaven.

*Matthew 5:14–16*

No one, when he has lit a lamp, puts it in a secret place or under a basket, but on a lampstand, that those who come in may see the light.

*Luke 11:33*

Finally, all of you be of one mind, having compassion for one another; love as brothers, be tenderhearted, be courteous;

not returning evil for evil or reviling for reviling, but on the contrary blessing, knowing that you were called to this, that you may inherit a blessing.

For

"He who would love life

And see good days,

Let him refrain his tongue from evil,

And his lips from speaking deceit.

Let him turn away from evil and do good;
Let him seek peace and pursue it."
But sanctify the Lord God in your hearts, and always be ready to give a defense to everyone who asks you a reason for the hope that is in you, with meekness and fear.

*1 Peter 3:8—11, 15*


Also I say to you, whoever confesses Me before men, him the Son of Man also will confess before the angels of God.
But he who denies Me before men will be denied before the angels of God.

*Luke 12:8—9*


Praying always with all prayer and supplication in the Spirit, being watchful to this end with all perseverance and supplication for all the saints—
and for me, that utterance may be given to me, that I may open my mouth boldly to make known the mystery of the gospel,
for which I am an ambassador in chains; that in it I may speak boldly, as I ought to speak.

*Ephesians 6:18—20*


Be diligent to present yourself approved to God, a worker who does not need to be ashamed, rightly dividing the word of truth.
But shun profane and idle babblings, for they will increase to more ungodliness.

But avoid foolish and ignorant disputes, knowing that they generate strife.

And a servant of the Lord must not quarrel but be gentle to all, able to teach, patient,

in humility correcting those who are in opposition, if God perhaps will grant them repentance, so that they may know the truth.

*2 Timothy 2:15–16, 23–25*


Good man out of the good treasure of his heart brings forth good; and an evil man out of the evil treasure of his heart brings forth evil. For out of the abundance of the heart his mouth speaks.

*Luke 6:45*


Therefore settle it in your hearts not to meditate beforehand on what you will answer;

for I will give you a mouth and wisdom which all your adversaries will not be able to contradict or resist.

*Luke 21:14–15*


By this all will know that you are My disciples, if you have love for one another.

*John 13:35*


What man of you, having a hundred sheep, if he loses one of them, does not leave the ninety-nine in the wilderness, and go after the one which is lost until he finds it?

And when he has found it, he lays it on his shoulders, rejoicing.

And when he comes home, he calls together his friends and neighbors, saying to them, "Rejoice with me, for I have found my sheep which was lost!"

I say to you that likewise there will be more joy in heaven over one sinner who repents than over ninety-nine just persons who need no repentance.

*Luke 15:4–7*


The fruit of the righteous is a tree of life,
And he who wins souls is wise.

*Proverbs 11:30*


Therefore do not be ashamed of the testimony of our Lord, nor of me His prisoner, but share with me in the sufferings for the gospel according to the power of God,

who has saved us and called us with a holy calling, not according to our works, but according to His own purpose and grace which was given to us in Christ Jesus before time began,

but has now been revealed by the appearing of our Savior Jesus Christ, who has abolished death and brought life and immortality to light through the gospel.

*2 Timothy 1:8–10*


I will sing to the LORD as long as I live;
I will sing praise to my God while I have my being.

*Psalm 104:33*

For God is my witness, whom I serve with my spirit in the gospel of His Son, that without ceasing I make mention of you always in my prayers . . .

For I am not ashamed of the gospel of Christ, for it is the power of God to salvation for everyone who believes, for the Jew first and also for the Greek.

For in it the righteousness of God is revealed from faith to faith; as it is written, "The just shall live by faith."

*Romans 1:9, 16–17*

Brethren, if anyone among you wanders from the truth, and someone turns him back,

let him know that he who turns a sinner from the error of his way will save a soul from death and cover a multitude of sins.

*James 5:19–20*

But you shall receive power when the Holy Spirit has come upon you; and you shall be witnesses to Me in Jerusalem, and in all Judea and Samaria, and to the end of the earth.

*Acts 1:8*

And He said to them, "Go into all the world and preach the gospel to every creature."

*Mark 16:15*

Then He said to them all, "If anyone desires to come after Me, let him deny himself, and take up his cross daily, and follow Me.

"For whoever desires to save his life will lose it, but whoever loses his life for My sake will save it.

For what profit is it to a man if he gains the whole world, and is himself destroyed or lost?

For whoever is ashamed of Me and My words, of him the Son of Man will be ashamed when He comes in His own glory, and in His Father's, and of the holy angels."

*Luke 9:23–26*


Preach the word! Be ready in season and out of season. Convince, rebuke, exhort, with all longsuffering and teaching.

*2 Timothy 4:2*


That I may proclaim with the voice of thanksgiving,
And tell of all Your wondrous works.

*Psalm 26:7*


Let the words of my mouth and the meditation of my heart
Be acceptable in Your sight,
O Lord, my strength and my Redeemer.

*Psalm 19:14*

# How to Handle Condemnation

Blessed are you when men hate you,
And when they exclude you,
And revile you, and cast out your name as evil,
For the Son of Man's sake.
Rejoice in that day and leap for joy!
For indeed your reward is great in heaven,
For in like manner their fathers did to the prophets.

*Luke 6:22–23*

If the world hates you, you know that it hated Me before it hated you.

If you were of the world, the world would love its own. Yet because you are not of the world, but I chose you out of the world, therefore the world hates you.

Remember the word that I said to you, "A servant is not greater than his master." If they persecuted Me, they will also persecute you. If they kept My word, they will keep yours also.

But all these things they will do to you for My name's sake, because they do not know Him who sent Me.

*John 15:18–21*

But even if you should suffer for righteousness' sake, you are blessed. "And do not be afraid of their threats, nor be troubled."

But sanctify the Lord God in your hearts, and always be ready to give a defense to everyone who asks you a reason for the hope that is in you, with meekness and fear;

having a good conscience, that when they defame you as evildoers, those who revile your good conduct in Christ may be ashamed.

*1 Peter 3:14—16*

If you are reproached for the name of Christ, blessed are you, for the Spirit of glory and of God rests upon you. On their part He is blasphemed, but on your part He is glorified.

Yet if anyone suffers as a Christian, let him not be ashamed, but let him glorify God in this matter.

*1 Peter 4:14, 16*

Cast out the scoffer, and contention will leave;
Yes, strife and reproach will cease.

*Proverbs 22:10*

Therefore, having been justified by faith, we have peace with God through our Lord Jesus Christ,

through whom also we have access by faith into this grace in which we stand, and rejoice in hope of the glory of God.

*Romans 5:1—2*

But the LORD has been my defense,
And my God the rock of my refuge.
He has brought on them their own iniquity,

And shall cut them off in their own wickedness;
The LORD our God shall cut them off.

*Psalm 94:22–23*

My eyes shall be on the faithful of the land,
That they may dwell with me;
He who walks in a perfect way,
He shall serve me.
He who works deceit shall not dwell within my house;
He who tells lies shall not continue in my presence.

*Psalm 101:6–7*

Do not say, "I will recompense evil";
Wait for the LORD, and He will save you.

*Proverbs 20:22*

By faith Moses, when he became of age, refused to be called the son of Pharaoh's daughter,
choosing rather to suffer affliction with the people of God than to enjoy the passing pleasures of sin,
esteeming the reproach of Christ greater riches than the treasures in Egypt; for he looked to the reward.

*Hebrews 11:24–26*

Therefore do not be ashamed of the testimony of our Lord, nor of me His prisoner, but share with me in the sufferings for the gospel according to the power of God,
who has saved us and called us with a holy calling, not

according to our works, but according to His own purpose and grace which was given to us in Christ Jesus before time began.

*2 Timothy 1:8–9*

Persecutions, afflictions, which happened to me at Antioch, at Iconium, at Lystra—what persecutions I endured. And out of them all the Lord delivered me.

Yes, and all who desire to live godly in Christ Jesus will suffer persecution.

*2 Timothy 3:11–12*

As it is written:
"There is none righteous, no, not one;
There is none who understands;
There is none who seeks after God.
They have all turned aside;
They have together become unprofitable;
There is none who does good, no, not one."

*Romans 3:10–12*

For this is commendable, if because of conscience toward God one endures grief, suffering wrongfully.

For what credit is it if, when you are beaten for your faults, you take it patiently? But when you do good and suffer, if you take it patiently, this is commendable before God.

For to this you were called, because Christ also suffered for us, leaving us an example, that you should follow His steps:
"Who committed no sin,
Nor was deceit found in His mouth";

who, when He was reviled, did not revile in return; when He suffered, He did not threaten, but committed Himself to Him who judges righteously;

who Himself bore our sins in His own body on the tree, that we, having died to sins, might live for righteousness— by whose stripes you were healed.

*1 Peter 2:19–24*

Behold, all those who were incensed against you
Shall be ashamed and disgraced;
They shall be as nothing,
And those who strive with you shall perish.
You shall seek them and not find them—
Those who contended with you.
Those who war against you
Shall be as nothing,
As a nonexistent thing.
For I, the LORD your God, will hold your right hand,
Saying to you, "Fear not, I will help you."

*Isaiah 41:11–13*

# What Is the Leading of the Lord?

The LORD will guide you continually,
And satisfy your soul in drought,
And strengthen your bones;
You shall be like a watered garden,
And like a spring of water, whose waters do not fail.

*Isaiah 58:11*

I say to you that likewise there will be more joy in heaven over one sinner who repents than over ninety-nine just persons who need no repentance.

*Luke 15:7*

"For My thoughts are not your thoughts,
Nor are your ways My ways," says the LORD.
"For as the heavens are higher than the earth,
So are My ways higher than your ways,
And My thoughts than your thoughts."

*Isaiah 55:8–9*

Beloved, do not believe every spirit, but test the spirits, whether they are of God; because many false prophets have gone out into the world.

*1 John 4:1*

The Lord is not slack concerning His promise, as some count slackness, but is longsuffering toward us, not willing that any should perish but that all should come to repentance.

*2 Peter 3:9*

For the Son of Man has come to save that which was lost.

*Matthew 18:11*

The spirit of a man is the lamp of the LORD,
Searching all the inner depths of his heart.

*Proverbs 20:27*

He found him in a desert land
And in the wasteland, a howling wilderness;
He encircled him, He instructed him,
He kept him as the apple of His eye.
As an eagle stirs up its nest,
Hovers over its young,
Spreading out its wings, taking them up,
Carrying them on its wings,
So the LORD alone led him,
And there was no foreign god with him.

*Deuteronomy 32:10–12*

So he shepherded them according to the integrity of his heart,
And guided them by the skillfulness of his hands.

*Psalm 78:72*

For you shall not go out with haste,
Nor go by flight;
For the LORD will go before you,
And the God of Israel will be your rear guard.

*Isaiah 52:12*


If a trumpet is blown in a city, will not the people be afraid?
If there is calamity in a city, will not the LORD have done it?
Surely the Lord GOD does nothing,
Unless He reveals His secret to His servants the prophets.
A lion has roared!
Who will not fear?
The Lord GOD has spoken!
Who can but prophesy?

*Amos 3:6–8*


By a prophet the LORD brought Israel out of Egypt,
And by a prophet he was preserved.

*Hosea 12:13*


For there are three that bear witness in heaven: the Father,
the Word, and the Holy Spirit; and these three are one.

*1 John 5:7*


Then He said, "Go out, and stand on the mountain before
the LORD." And behold, the LORD passed by, and a great and
strong wind tore into the mountains and broke the rocks in
pieces before the LORD, but the LORD was not in the wind;

and after the wind an earthquake, but the LORD was not in the earthquake;

and after the earthquake a fire, but the LORD was not in the fire; and after the fire a still small voice.

*1 Kings 19:11–12*


A man's heart plans his way,
But the LORD directs his steps.
The lot is cast into the lap,
But its every decision is from the LORD.

*Proverbs 16:9, 33*

# How to Wait on God

Rest in the LORD, and wait patiently for Him;
Do not fret because of him who prospers in his way,
Because of the man who brings wicked schemes to pass.
Cease from anger, and forsake wrath;
Do not fret—it only causes harm.
For evildoers shall be cut off;
But those who wait on the LORD,
They shall inherit the earth.

*Psalm 37:7–9*


I waited patiently for the LORD;
And He inclined to me,
And heard my cry.
He also brought me up out of a horrible pit,
Out of the miry clay,
And set my feet upon a rock,
And established my steps.
He has put a new song in my mouth—
Praise to our God;
Many will see it and fear,
And will trust in the LORD.

*Psalm 40:1–3*

Therefore the LORD will wait, that He may be gracious to you;

And therefore He will be exalted, that He may have mercy on you.

For the LORD is a God of justice;

Blessed are all those who wait for Him.

*Isaiah 30:18*

Indeed, let no one who waits on You be ashamed;

Let those be ashamed who deal treacherously without cause.

Show me Your ways, O LORD;

Teach me Your paths.

Lead me in Your truth and teach me,

For You are the God of my salvation;

On You I wait all the day.

Let integrity and uprightness preserve me,

For I wait for You.

*Psalm 25:3–5, 21*

Wait on the LORD;

Be of good courage,

And He shall strengthen your heart;

Wait, I say, on the LORD!

*Psalm 27:14*

But those who wait on the LORD

Shall renew their strength;

They shall mount up with wings like eagles,

They shall run and not be weary,
They shall walk and not faint.

*Isaiah 40:31*

The LORD is good to those who wait for Him,
To the soul who seeks Him.
It is good that one should hope and wait quietly
For the salvation of the LORD.

*Lamentations 3:25–26*

Therefore I will look to the LORD;
I will wait for the God of my salvation;
My God will hear me.

*Micah 7:7*

And you yourselves be like men who wait for their master, when he will return from the wedding, that when he comes and knocks they may open to him immediately.

*Luke 12:36*

For they themselves declare concerning us what manner of entry we had to you, and how you turned to God from idols to serve the living and true God,

and to wait for His Son from heaven, whom He raised from the dead, even Jesus who delivers us from the wrath to come.

*1 Thessalonians 1:9–10*

My soul, wait silently for God alone,
For my expectation is from Him.
He only is my rock and my salvation;
He is my defense;
I shall not be moved.

*Psalm 62:5–6*

I have waited for your salvation, O LORD!

*Genesis 49:18*

The LORD upholds all who fall,
And raises up all who are bowed down.
The eyes of all look expectantly to You,
And You give them their food in due season.

*Psalm 145:14–15*

And now, Lord, what do I wait for?
My hope is in You.
Deliver me from all my transgressions;
Do not make me the reproach of the foolish.

*Psalm 39:7–8*

They soon forgot His works;
They did not wait for His counsel.

*Psalm 106:13*

I wait for the LORD, my soul waits,
And in His word I do hope.

My soul waits for the Lord
More than those who watch for the morning—
Yes, more than those who watch for the morning.

*Psalm 130:5–6*


And it will be said in that day:
"Behold, this is our God;
We have waited for Him, and He will save us.
This is the LORD;
We have waited for Him;
We will be glad and rejoice in His salvation."

*Isaiah 25:9*


Kings shall be your foster fathers,
And their queens your nursing mothers;
They shall bow down to you with their faces to the earth,
And lick up the dust of your feet.
Then you will know that I am the LORD,
For they shall not be ashamed who wait for Me.

*Isaiah 49:23*


For since the beginning of the world
Men have not heard nor perceived by the ear,
Nor has the eye seen any God besides You,
Who acts for the one who waits for Him.

*Isaiah 64:4*

For the Egyptians shall help in vain and to no purpose.
Therefore I have called her Rahab-Hem-Shebeth.

*Isaiah 30:7*

Let us hold fast the confession of our hope without wavering, for He who promised is faithful.

*Hebrews 10:23*

So you, by the help of your God, return;
Observe mercy and justice,
And wait on your God continually.

*Hosea 12:6*

# What Is the Importance of Obedience?

That all the peoples of the earth may know that the LORD is God; there is no other.

Let your heart therefore be loyal to the LORD our God, to walk in His statutes and keep His commandments, as at this day.

*1 Kings 8:60–61*

But be doers of the word, and not hearers only, deceiving yourselves.

*James 1:22*

Now therefore, if you will indeed obey My voice and keep My covenant, then you shall be a special treasure to Me above all people; for all the earth is Mine.

*Exodus 19:5*

Do not be deceived, God is not mocked; for whatever a man sows, that he will also reap.

For he who sows to his flesh will of the flesh reap corruption, but he who sows to the Spirit will of the Spirit reap everlasting life.

*Galatians 6:7–8*

If you love Me, keep My commandments.

*John 14:15*

Whoever comes to Me, and hears My sayings and does them, I will show you whom he is like:

He is like a man building a house, who dug deep and laid the foundation on the rock. And when the flood arose, the stream beat vehemently against that house, and could not shake it, for it was founded on the rock.

But he who heard and did nothing is like a man who built a house on the earth without a foundation, against which the stream beat vehemently; and immediately it fell. And the ruin of that house was great.

*Luke 6:47–49*

Do you see that faith was working together with his works, and by works faith was made perfect?

And the Scripture was fulfilled which says, "Abraham believed God, and it was accounted to him for righteousness." And he was called the friend of God.

*James 2:22–23*

But Peter and the other apostles answered and said: "We ought to obey God rather than men."

*Acts 5:29*

For if there is first a willing mind, it is accepted according to what one has, and not according to what he does not have.

And not only that, but who was also chosen by the churches

to travel with us with this gift, which is administered by us to the glory of the Lord Himself and to show your ready mind.

*2 Corinthians 8:12, 19*

But Jesus called them to Him and said, "Let the little children come to Me, and do not forbid them; for of such is the kingdom of God.

Assuredly, I say to you, whoever does not receive the kingdom of God as a little child will by no means enter it."

*Luke 18:16–17*

But I discipline my body and bring it into subjection, lest, when I have preached to others, I myself should become disqualified.

*1 Corinthians 9:27*

Casting down arguments and every high thing that exalts itself against the knowledge of God, bringing every thought into captivity to the obedience of Christ.

*2 Corinthians 10:5*

Furthermore, we have had human fathers who corrected us, and we paid them respect. Shall we not much more readily be in subjection to the Father of spirits and live?

For they indeed for a few days chastened us as seemed best to them, but He for our profit, that we may be partakers of His holiness.

*Hebrews 12:9–10*

Whoever has no rule over his own spirit
Is like a city broken down, without walls.

*Proverbs 25:28*


He who is faithful in what is least is faithful also in much;
and he who is unjust in what is least is unjust also in much.

*Luke 16:10*


But we see Jesus, who was made a little lower than the
angels, for the suffering of death crowned with glory and
honor, that He, by the grace of God, might taste death for
everyone.

For it was fitting for Him, for whom are all things and by
whom are all things, in bringing many sons to glory, to make
the captain of their salvation perfect through sufferings.

*Hebrews 2:9–10*


Behold, You desire truth in the inward parts,
And in the hidden part You will make me to know wisdom.

*Psalm 51:6*


When He had called the people to Himself, with His disciples also, He said to them, "Whoever desires to come after Me,
let him deny himself, and take up his cross, and follow Me.

For whoever desires to save his life will lose it, but whoever
loses his life for My sake and the gospel's will save it.

For what will it profit a man if he gains the whole world,
and loses his own soul?

Or what will a man give in exchange for his soul?"

*Mark 8:34–37*

And the world is passing away, and the lust of it; but he who does the will of God abides forever.

*1 John 2:17*

So rend your heart, and not your garments;
Return to the Lord your God,
For He is gracious and merciful,
Slow to anger, and of great kindness;
And He relents from doing harm.

*Joel 2:13*

If anyone does not abide in Me, he is cast out as a branch and is withered; and they gather them and throw them into the fire, and they are burned.

If you abide in Me, and My words abide in you, you will ask what you desire, and it shall be done for you.

If you keep My commandments, you will abide in My love, just as I have kept My Father's commandments and abide in His love.

*John 15:6–7, 10*

If you forsake the Lord and serve foreign gods, then He will turn and do you harm and consume you, after He has done you good.

*Joshua 24:20*

Now the LORD was with Jehoshaphat, because he walked in the former ways of his father David; he did not seek the Baals,

but sought the God of his father, and walked in His commandments and not according to the acts of Israel.

*2 Chronicles 17:3–4*

Now the just shall live by faith;
But if anyone draws back,
My soul has no pleasure in him.

*Hebrews 10:38*

So Samuel said:
"Has the LORD as great delight in burnt offerings and sacrifices,
As in obeying the voice of the LORD?
Behold, to obey is better than sacrifice,
And to heed than the fat of rams."

*1 Samuel 15:22*

If you are willing and obedient,
You shall eat the good of the land;
But if you refuse and rebel,
You shall be devoured by the sword;
For the mouth of the LORD has spoken.

*Isaiah 1:19–20*

# HOW TO GIVE TO GOD'S WORK

Do not lay up for yourselves treasures on earth, where moth and rust destroy and where thieves break in and steal;

but lay up for yourselves treasures in heaven, where neither moth nor rust destroys and where thieves do not break in and steal.

For where your treasure is, there your heart will be also.

*Matthew 6:19–21*

Now Jesus sat opposite the treasury and saw how the people put money into the treasury. And many who were rich put in much.

Then one poor widow came and threw in two mites, which make a quadrans.

So He called His disciples to Himself and said to them, "Assuredly, I say to you that this poor widow has put in more than all those who have given to the treasury;

for they all put in out of their abundance, but she out of her poverty put in all that she had, her whole livelihood."

*Mark 12:41–44*

But this I say: He who sows sparingly will also reap sparingly, and he who sows bountifully will also reap bountifully.

So let each one give as he purposes in his heart, not grudgingly or of necessity; for God loves a cheerful giver.

*2 Corinthians 9:6–7*

When you make a vow to God, do not delay to pay it;
For He has no pleasure in fools.
Pay what you have vowed—
Better not to vow than to vow and not pay.
Do not let your mouth cause your flesh to sin, nor say before the messenger of God that it was an error. Why should God be angry at your excuse and destroy the work of your hands?

*Ecclesiastes 5:4–6*

Give to the LORD the glory due His name;
Bring an offering, and come before Him.
Oh, worship the LORD in the beauty of holiness!

*1 Chronicles 16:29*

Therefore, when you do a charitable deed, do not sound a trumpet before you as the hypocrites do in the synagogues and in the streets, that they may have glory from men. Assuredly, I say to you, they have their reward.

But when you do a charitable deed, do not let your left hand know what your right hand is doing,

that your charitable deed may be in secret; and your Father who sees in secret will Himself reward you openly.

*Matthew 6:2–4*

Again, the kingdom of heaven is like treasure hidden in a field, which a man found and hid; and for joy over it he goes and sells all that he has and buys that field.

Again, the kingdom of heaven is like a merchant seeking beautiful pearls,

who, when he had found one pearl of great price, went and sold all that he had and bought it.

*Matthew 13:44–46*

On the first day of the week let each one of you lay something aside, storing up as he may prosper, that there be no collections when I come.

*1 Corinthians 16:2*

And Elijah said to her, "Do not fear; go and do as you have said, but make me a small cake from it first, and bring it to me; and afterward make some for yourself and your son.

For thus says the LORD God of Israel: 'The bin of flour shall not be used up, nor shall the jar of oil run dry, until the day the LORD sends rain on the earth.'"

*1 Kings 17:13–14*

Then the people rejoiced, for they had offered willingly, because with a loyal heart they had offered willingly to the LORD; and King David also rejoiced greatly.

*1 Chronicles 29:9*

Give to the LORD the glory due His name;
Bring an offering, and come into His courts.

*Psalm 96:8*


There is one who scatters, yet increases more;
And there is one who withholds more than is right,
But it leads to poverty.
The generous soul will be made rich,
And he who waters will also be watered himself.

*Proverbs 11:24–25*


He who has a generous eye will be blessed,
For he gives of his bread to the poor.

*Proverbs 22:9*


The righteous considers the cause of the poor,
But the wicked does not understand such knowledge.

*Proverbs 29:7*


Cast your bread upon the waters,
For you will find it after many days.

*Ecclesiastes 11:1*


Take from among you an offering to the LORD. Whoever
is of a willing heart, let him bring it as an offering to the
LORD: gold, silver, and bronze.

*Exodus 35:5*

So rend your heart, and not your garments;
Return to the LORD your God,
For He is gracious and merciful,
Slow to anger, and of great kindness;
And He relents from doing harm.
Who knows if He will turn and relent,
And leave a blessing behind Him—
A grain offering and a drink offering
For the LORD your God?

*Joel 2:13—14*


But woe to you Pharisees! For you tithe mint and rue and all manner of herbs, and pass by justice and the love of God. These you ought to have done, without leaving the others undone.

*Luke 11:42*


As it is written, "He who gathered much had nothing left over, and he who gathered little had no lack."

*2 Corinthians 8:15*


He who is faithful in what is least is faithful also in much; and he who is unjust in what is least is unjust also in much.
Therefore if you have not been faithful in the unrighteous mammon, who will commit to your trust the true riches?

*Luke 16:10—11*


Therefore bear fruits worthy of repentance,
and do not think to say to yourselves, "We have Abraham

as our father." For I say to you that God is able to raise up children to Abraham from these stones.

*Matthew 3:8—9*

Does he thank that servant because he did the things that were commanded him? I think not.

So likewise you, when you have done all those things which you are commanded, say, "We are unprofitable servants. We have done what was our duty to do."

*Luke 17:9—10*

As soon as the commandment was circulated, the children of Israel brought in abundance the firstfruits of grain and wine, oil and honey, and of all the produce of the field; and they brought in abundantly the tithe of everything.

*2 Chronicles 31:5*

# HOPING
# IN CHRIST

# How to Commit Your Life to Christ

That if you confess with your mouth the Lord Jesus and believe in your heart that God has raised Him from the dead, you will be saved.

For with the heart one believes unto righteousness, and with the mouth confession is made unto salvation.

For the Scripture says, "Whoever believes on Him will not be put to shame."

For there is no distinction between Jew and Greek, for the same Lord over all is rich to all who call upon Him.

For "whoever calls on the name of the LORD shall be saved."

*Romans 10:9–13*

Trust in the LORD, and do good;
Dwell in the land, and feed on His faithfulness.
Delight yourself also in the LORD,
And He shall give you the desires of your heart.
Commit your way to the LORD,
Trust also in Him,
And He shall bring it to pass.
He shall bring forth your righteousness as the light,
And your justice as the noonday.
Rest in the LORD, and wait patiently for Him;

Do not fret because of him who prospers in his way,
Because of the man who brings wicked schemes to pass.

*Psalm 37:3–7*


Seek the LORD while He may be found,
Call upon Him while He is near.
Let the wicked forsake his way,
And the unrighteous man his thoughts;
Let him return to the LORD,
And He will have mercy on him;
And to our God,
For He will abundantly pardon.

*Isaiah 55:6–7*


Behold, I stand at the door and knock. If anyone hears My voice and opens the door, I will come in to him and dine with him, and he with Me.

*Revelation 3:20*


All that the Father gives Me will come to Me, and the one who comes to Me I will by no means cast out.

And this is the will of Him who sent Me, that everyone who sees the Son and believes in Him may have everlasting life; and I will raise him up at the last day.

No one can come to Me unless the Father who sent Me draws him; and I will raise him up at the last day.

It is written in the prophets, "And they shall all be taught by God." Therefore everyone who has heard and learned from the Father comes to Me.

Not that anyone has seen the Father, except He who is from God; He has seen the Father.

Most assuredly, I say to you, he who believes in Me has everlasting life.

*John 6:37, 40, 44–47*

But without faith it is impossible to please Him, for he who comes to God must believe that He is, and that He is a rewarder of those who diligently seek Him.

*Hebrews 11:6*

I will give you a new heart and put a new spirit within you; I will take the heart of stone out of your flesh and give you a heart of flesh.

I will put My Spirit within you and cause you to walk in My statutes, and you will keep My judgments and do them.

*Ezekiel 36:26–27*

The Lord is not slack concerning His promise, as some count slackness, but is longsuffering toward us, not willing that any should perish but that all should come to repentance.

but grow in the grace and knowledge of our Lord and Savior Jesus Christ. To Him be the glory both now and forever. Amen.

*2 Peter 3:9, 18*

Draw near to God and He will draw near to you. Cleanse your hands, you sinners; and purify your hearts, you double-minded.

*James 4:8*

But now having been set free from sin, and having become slaves of God, you have your fruit to holiness, and the end, everlasting life.

For the wages of sin is death, but the gift of God is eternal life in Christ Jesus our Lord.

*Romans 6:22—23*


Have mercy upon me, O God,
According to Your lovingkindness;
According to the multitude of
Your tender mercies,
Blot out my transgressions.
Wash me thoroughly from my iniquity,
And cleanse me from my sin.
For I acknowledge my transgressions,
And my sin is always before me.
Create in me a clean heart, O God,
And renew a steadfast spirit within me.
Do not cast me away from Your presence,
And do not take Your Holy Spirit from me.
Restore to me the joy of Your salvation,
And uphold me by Your generous Spirit.

*Psalm 51:1—3, 10—12*


For this reason I also suffer these things; nevertheless I am not ashamed, for I know whom I have believed and am persuaded that He is able to keep what I have committed to Him until that Day.

*2 Timothy 1:12*

Therefore whoever confesses Me before men, him I will also confess before My Father who is in heaven.

And he who does not take his cross and follow after Me is not worthy of Me.

He who finds his life will lose it, and he who loses his life for My sake will find it.

He who receives you receives Me, and he who receives Me receives Him who sent Me.

He who receives a prophet in the name of a prophet shall receive a prophet's reward. And he who receives a righteous man in the name of a righteous man shall receive a righteous man's reward.

And whoever gives one of these little ones only a cup of cold water in the name of a disciple, assuredly, I say to you, he shall by no means lose his reward.

*Matthew 10:32, 38–42*

Come now, you who say, "Today or tomorrow we will go to such and such a city, spend a year there, buy and sell, and make a profit";

whereas you do not know what will happen tomorrow. For what is your life? It is even a vapor that appears for a little time and then vanishes away.

Instead you ought to say, "If the Lord wills, we shall live and do this or that."

*James 4:13–15*

I tell you, no; but unless you repent you will all likewise perish.

*Luke 13:3*

# HOW TO DRAW NIGH TO GOD

Draw near to God and He will draw near to you. Cleanse your hands, you sinners; and purify your hearts, you double-minded.

Lament and mourn and weep! Let your laughter be turned to mourning and your joy to gloom.

Humble yourselves in the sight of the Lord, and He will lift you up.

*James 4:8–10*

I love those who love me,
And those who seek Me diligently will find me.

*Proverbs 8:17*

So I say to you, ask, and it will be given to you; seek, and you will find; knock, and it will be opened to you.

For everyone who asks receives, and he who seeks finds, and to him who knocks it will be opened.

If a son asks for bread from any father among you, will he give him a stone? Or if he asks for a fish, will he give him a serpent instead of a fish?

Or if he asks for an egg, will he offer him a scorpion?

If you then, being evil, know how to give good gifts to your children, how much more will your heavenly Father give the Holy Spirit to those who ask Him!

*Luke 11:9–13*

Seek the Lord and His strength;
Seek His face evermore!
Remember His marvelous works which He has done,
His wonders, and the judgments of His mouth.

*1 Chronicles 16:11–12*

Then you will call upon Me and go and pray to Me, and I will listen to you.

And you will seek Me and find Me, when you search for Me with all your heart.

*Jeremiah 29:12–13*

As the deer pants for the water brooks,
So pants my soul for You, O God.
My soul thirsts for God, for the living God.
When shall I come and appear before God?
Deep calls unto deep at the noise of Your waterfalls;
All Your waves and billows have gone over me.
The LORD will command His lovingkindness in the day-time,
And in the night his song shall be with me—
A prayer to the God of my life.

*Psalm 42:1–2, 7–8*

Blessed are those who keep His testimonies,
Who seek Him with the whole heart!
With my whole heart I have sought You;
Oh, let me not wander from Your commandments!

*Psalm 119:2, 10*

I wait for the LORD, my soul waits,
And in His word I do hope.
My soul waits for the Lord
More than those who watch for the morning—
Yes, more than those who watch for the morning.

*Psalm 130:5–6*

The LORD is near to all who call upon Him,
To all who call upon Him in truth.

*Psalm 145:18*

In my distress I called upon the LORD,
And cried out to my God;
He heard my voice from His temple,
And my cry came before Him, even to His ears.

*Psalm 18:6*

In the day when I cried out, You answered me,
And made me bold with strength in my soul.

*Psalm 138:3*

Thus I will bless You while I live;
I will lift up my hands in Your name.

My soul shall be satisfied as with marrow and fatness,
And my mouth shall praise You with joyful lips.

*Psalm 63:4–5*


My soul, wait silently for God alone,
For my expectation is from Him.

*Psalm 62:5*


Hear my cry, O God;
Attend to my prayer.
From the end of the earth I will cry to You,
When my heart is overwhelmed;
Lead me to the rock that is higher than I.

*Psalm 61:1–2*

# How to Recover Spiritually

Have you not known?
Have you not heard?
The everlasting God, the LORD,
The Creator of the ends of the earth,
Neither faints nor is weary.
His understanding is unsearchable.
He gives power to the weak,
And to those who have no might he increases strength.
But those who wait on the LORD
Shall renew their strength;
They shall mount up with wings like eagles,
They shall run and not be weary,
They shall walk and not faint.

*Isaiah 40:28—29, 31*

Brethren, I do not count myself to have apprehended; but one thing I do, forgetting those things which are behind and reaching forward to those things which are ahead,

I press toward the goal for the prize of the upward call of God in Christ Jesus.

*Philippians 3:13—14*

For You, Lord, are good, and ready to forgive,
And abundant in mercy to all those who call upon You.
Give ear, O LORD, to my prayer;
And attend to the voice of my supplications.
In the day of my trouble I will call upon You,
For You will answer me.

*Psalm 86:5–7*

"I will seek what was lost and bring back what was driven away, bind up the broken and strengthen what was sick; but I will destroy the fat and the strong, and feed them in judgment.

Thus they shall know that I, the LORD their God, am with them, and they, the house of Israel, are My people," says the Lord GOD.

"You are My flock, the flock of My pasture; you are men, and I am your God," says the Lord GOD.

*Ezekiel 34:16, 30–31*

He who covers his sins will not prosper,
But whoever confesses and forsakes them will have mercy.

*Proverbs 28:13*

Before I was afflicted I went astray,
But now I keep Your word.
You are good, and do good;
Teach me Your statutes.

*Psalm 119:67–68*

Now no chastening seems to be joyful for the present, but painful; nevertheless, afterward it yields the peaceable fruit of righteousness to those who have been trained by it.

Therefore strengthen the hands which hang down, and the feeble knees,

and make straight paths for your feet, so that what is lame may not be dislocated, but rather be healed.

Pursue peace with all people, and holiness, without which no one will see the Lord.

*Hebrews 12:11—14*

Take away the dross from silver,
And it will go to the silversmith for jewelry.

*Proverbs 25:4*

The righteous shall flourish like a palm tree,
He shall grow like a cedar in Lebanon.
Those who are planted in the house of the LORD
Shall flourish in the courts of our God.
They shall still bear fruit in old age;
They shall be fresh and flourishing,
To declare that the LORD is upright;
He is my rock, and there is no unrighteousness in Him.

*Psalm 92:12—15*

Blessed is the man whom You instruct, O LORD,
And teach out of Your law,
That You may give him rest from the days of adversity,
Until the pit is dug for the wicked.

For the LORD will not cast off His people,
Nor will He forsake His inheritance.

*Psalm 94:12–14*


I will heal their backsliding,
I will love them freely,
For My anger has turned away from him.

*Hosea 14:4*


Poverty and shame will come to him who disdains correction,
But he who regards a rebuke will be honored.

*Proverbs 13:18*


But, speaking the truth in love, may grow up in all things into Him who is the head—Christ—
from whom the whole body, joined and knit together by what every joint supplies, according to the effective working by which every part does its share, causes growth of the body for the edifying of itself in love.

*Ephesians 4:15–16*


When my soul fainted within me,
I remembered the LORD;
And my prayer went up to You,
Into Your holy temple.
"Those who regard worthless idols
Forsake their own mercy.
But I will sacrifice to You

With the voice of thanksgiving;
I will pay what I have vowed.
Salvation is of the LORD."

*Jonah 2:7–9*

# How to Obtain the Promises

By which have been given to us exceedingly great and precious promises, that through these you may be partakers of the divine nature, having escaped the corruption that is in the world through lust.

But also for this very reason, giving all diligence, add to your faith virtue, to virtue knowledge,

to knowledge self-control, to self-control perseverance, to perseverance godliness,

to godliness brotherly kindness, and to brotherly kindness love.

For if these things are yours and abound, you will be neither barren nor unfruitful in the knowledge of our Lord Jesus Christ.

*2 Peter 1:4–8*

Let us hold fast the confession of our hope without wavering, for He who promised is faithful.

Therefore do not cast away your confidence, which has great reward.

For you have need of endurance, so that after you have done the will of God, you may receive the promise:

"For yet a little while,
And He who is coming will come and will not tarry."

*Hebrews 10:23, 35–37*

For if you carefully keep all these commandments which I command you to do—to love the LORD your God, to walk in all His ways, and to hold fast to Him—

then the LORD will drive out all these nations from before you, and you will dispossess greater and mightier nations than yourselves.

*Deuteronomy 11:22–23*

Only be strong and very courageous, that you may observe to do according to all the law which Moses My servant commanded you; do not turn from it to the right hand or to the left, that you may prosper wherever you go.

*Joshua 1:7*

For assuredly, I say to you, whoever says to this mountain, "Be removed and be cast into the sea," and does not doubt in his heart, but believes that those things he says will be done, he will have whatever he says.

*Mark 11:23*

Now faith is the substance of things hoped for, the evidence of things not seen.

But without faith it is impossible to please Him, for he

who comes to God must believe that He is, and that He is a rewarder of those who diligently seek Him.

By faith Sarah herself also received strength to conceive seed, and she bore a child when she was past the age, because she judged Him faithful who had promised.

*Hebrews 11:1, 6, 11*

That you do not become sluggish, but imitate those who through faith and patience inherit the promises.

*Hebrews 6:12*

For you are all sons of God through faith in Christ Jesus.

For as many of you as were baptized into Christ have put on Christ.

There is neither Jew nor Greek, there is neither slave nor free, there is neither male nor female; for you are all one in Christ Jesus.

And if you are Christ's, then you are Abraham's seed, and heirs according to the promise.

*Galatians 3:26–29*

If you are willing and obedient,
You shall eat the good of the land;
But if you refuse and rebel,
You shall be devoured by the sword;
For the mouth of the LORD has spoken.

*Isaiah 1:19–20*

Therefore it is of faith that it might be according to grace, so that the promise might be sure to all the seed, not only to those who are of the law, but also to those who are of the faith of Abraham, who is the father of us all.

*Romans 4:16*

Now this is the confidence that we have in Him, that if we ask anything according to His will, He hears us.

And if we know that He hears us, whatever we ask, we know that we have the petitions that we have asked of Him.

*1 John 5:14–15*

And said, "If you diligently heed the voice of the LORD your God and do what is right in His sight, give ear to His commandments and keep all His statutes, I will put none of the diseases on you which I have brought on the Egyptians. For I am the LORD who heals you."

*Exodus 15:26*

If any of you lacks wisdom, let him ask of God, who gives to all liberally and without reproach, and it will be given to him.

But let him ask in faith, with no doubting, for he who doubts is like a wave of the sea driven and tossed by the wind.

For let not that man suppose that he will receive anything from the Lord;

he is a double-minded man, unstable in all his ways.

*James 1:5–8*

Behold, the LORD's hand is not shortened,
That it cannot save;
Nor His ear heavy,
That it cannot hear.
But your iniquities have separated you from your God;
And your sins have hidden His face from you,
So that He will not hear.

*Isaiah 59:1–2*


But seek first the kingdom of God and His righteousness, and all these things shall be added to you.

*Matthew 6:33*

# UNDERSTANDING
# IN CHRIST

# HOW TO UNDERSTAND
# THE PERSONALITY OF GOD

As for God, His way is perfect;
The word of the LORD is proven;
He is a shield to all who trust in Him.
For who is God, except the LORD?
And who is a rock, except our God?
It is God who arms me with strength,
And makes my way perfect.

*Psalm 18:30–32*

"For My thoughts are not your thoughts,
Nor are your ways My ways," says the LORD.
"For as the heavens are higher than the earth,
So are My ways higher than your ways,
And My thoughts than your thoughts."

*Isaiah 55:8–9*

Though the LORD is on high,
Yet He regards the lowly;
But the proud He knows from afar.
Though I walk in the midst of trouble,
You will revive me;
You will stretch out Your hand

Against the wrath of my enemies,
And Your right hand will save me.

*Psalm 138:6–7*

Every good gift and every perfect gift is from above, and comes down from the Father of lights, with whom there is no variation or shadow of turning.

*James 1:17*

I, the LORD, search the heart,
I test the mind,
Even to give every man according to his ways,
According to the fruit of his doings.

*Jeremiah 17:10*

He has made the earth by His power,
He has established the world by His wisdom,
And has stretched out the heavens at His discretion.

*Jeremiah 10:12*

The LORD is in His holy temple,
The LORD's throne is in heaven;
His eyes behold,
His eyelids test the sons of men.
The LORD tests the righteous,
But the wicked and the one who loves violence His soul hates.
For the LORD is righteous,

He loves righteousness;
His countenance beholds the upright.

*Psalm 11:4–5, 7*

Now therefore, let the fear of the LORD be upon you; take care and do it, for there is no iniquity with the LORD our God, no partiality, nor taking of bribes.

*2 Chronicles 19:7*

I know that You can do everything,
And that no purpose of Yours can be withheld from You.

*Job 42:2*

And all the trees of the field shall know that I, the LORD, have brought down the high tree and exalted the low tree, dried up the green tree and made the dry tree flourish; I, the LORD, have spoken and have done it.

*Ezekiel 17:24*

Jesus said to them, "Have you never read in the Scriptures:
'The stone which the builders rejected
has become the chief cornerstone.
This was the LORD's doing,
And it is marvelous in our eyes'?"

*Matthew 21:42*

As a father pities his children,
So the LORD pities those who fear Him.

For He knows our frame;
He remembers that we are dust.

*Psalm 103:13—14*


If you then, being evil, know how to give good gifts to your children, how much more will your Father who is in heaven give good things to those who ask Him!

*Matthew 7:11*


But glory, honor, and peace to everyone who works what is good, to the Jew first and also to the Greek.

For there is no partiality with God.

*Romans 2:10—11*


Because the foolishness of God is wiser than men, and the weakness of God is stronger than men.

*1 Corinthians 1:25*


Great is our Lord, and mighty in power;
His understanding is infinite.

*Psalm 147:5*


Great is the LORD, and greatly to be praised;
And His greatness is unsearchable.
The LORD is gracious and full of compassion,
Slow to anger and great in mercy.
The LORD is good to all,
And His tender mercies are over all His works.

*Psalm 145:3, 8—9*

Therefore, since we are receiving a kingdom which cannot be shaken, let us have grace, by which we may serve God acceptably with reverence and godly fear.

For our God is a consuming fire.

*Hebrews 12:28–29*

If we confess our sins, He is faithful and just to forgive us our sins and to cleanse us from all unrighteousness.

*1 John 1:9*

For His anger is but for a moment,
His favor is for life;
Weeping may endure for a night,
But joy comes in the morning.

*Psalm 30:5*

So he shepherded them according to the integrity of his heart,
And guided them by the skillfulness of his hands.

*Psalm 78:72*

After that, He poured water into a basin and began to wash the disciples' feet, and to wipe them with the towel with which He was girded.

"If I then, your Lord and Teacher, have washed your feet, you also ought to wash one another's feet."

*John 13:5, 14*

# How to Receive Understanding

The fear of the LORD is the beginning of wisdom;
A good understanding have all those who do His commandments.
His praise endures forever.

*Psalm 111:10*

Counsel is mine, and sound wisdom;
I am understanding, I have strength.

*Proverbs 8:14*

Understanding is a wellspring of life to him who has it.
But the correction of fools is folly.

*Proverbs 16:22*

Forsake foolishness and live,
And go in the way of understanding.
The fear of the LORD is the beginning of wisdom,
And the knowledge of the Holy One is understanding.

*Proverbs 9:6, 10*

How much better to get wisdom than gold!
And to get understanding is to be chosen rather than silver.

The highway of the upright is to depart from evil;
He who keeps his way preserves his soul.

*Proverbs 16:16–17*

Surely the Lord GOD does nothing,
Unless He reveals His secret to His servants the prophets.
A lion has roared!
Who will not fear?
The Lord GOD has spoken!
Who can but prophesy?

*Amos 3:7–8*

If any of you lacks wisdom, let him ask of God, who gives to all liberally and without reproach, and it will be given to him.

*James 1:5*

Make me understand the way of Your precepts;
So shall I meditate on Your wonderful works.
Give me understanding, and I shall keep Your law;
Indeed, I shall observe it with my whole heart.
Your hands have made me and fashioned me;
Give me understanding, that I may learn Your commandments.
You, through Your commandments, make me wiser than my enemies;
For they are ever with me.
Through Your precepts I get understanding;
Therefore I hate every false way.

Your word is a lamp to my feet
And a light to my path.
I am your servant;
Give me understanding,
That I may know Your testimonies.

*Psalm 119:27, 34, 73, 98, 104—105, 125*

Yes, if you cry out for discernment,
And lift up your voice for understanding,
If you seek her as silver,
And search for her as for hidden treasures;
Then you will understand the fear of the LORD,
And find the knowledge of God.
For the LORD gives wisdom;
From His mouth come knowledge and understanding;
He stores up sound wisdom for the upright;
He is a shield to those who walk uprightly;
He guards the paths of justice,
And preserves the way of His saints.
Then you will understand righteousness and justice,
Equity and every good path.
When wisdom enters your heart,
And knowledge is pleasant to your soul,
Discretion will preserve you;
Understanding will keep you.

*Proverbs 2:3—11*

Get wisdom! Get understanding!
Do not forget, nor turn away from the words of my mouth.

Do not forsake her, and she will preserve you;
Love her, and she will keep you.
Wisdom is the principal thing;
Therefore get wisdom.
And in all your getting, get understanding.

*Proverbs 4:5–7*

The heart of him who has understanding seeks knowledge,
But the mouth of fools feeds on foolishness.
Folly is joy to him who is destitute of discernment,
But a man of understanding walks uprightly.
He who disdains instruction despises his own soul,
But he who heeds rebuke gets understanding.
The fear of the LORD is the instruction of wisdom,
And before honor is humility.

*Proverbs 15:14, 21, 32–33*

For what man knows the things of a man except the spirit of the man which is in him? Even so no one knows the things of God except the Spirit of God.

Now we have received, not the spirit of the world, but the Spirit who is from God, that we might know the things that have been freely given to us by God.

These things we also speak, not in words which man's wisdom teaches but which the Holy Spirit teaches, comparing spiritual things with spiritual.

*1 Corinthians 2:11–13*

Incline your ear, and come to Me.
Hear, and your soul shall live;
And I will make an everlasting covenant with you—
The sure mercies of David.
Seek the LORD while He may be found,
Call upon Him while He is near.
"For My thoughts are not your thoughts,
Nor are your ways My ways," says the LORD.
"For as the heavens are higher than the earth,
So are My ways higher than your ways,
And My thoughts than your thoughts."

*Isaiah 55:3, 6, 8–9*

But there is a spirit in man,
And the breath of the Almighty gives him understanding.

*Job 32:8*

# WHAT IS THE FEAR OF THE LORD?

The LORD is righteous in all His ways,
Gracious in all His works.
The LORD is near to all who call upon Him,
To all who call upon Him in truth.
He will fulfill the desire of those who fear Him;
He also will hear their cry and save them.

*Psalm 145:17–19*

He does not delight in the strength of the horse;
He takes no pleasure in the legs of a man.
The LORD takes pleasure in those who fear Him,
In those who hope in His mercy.

*Psalm 147:10–11*

If you seek her as silver,
And search for her as for hidden treasures;
Then you will understand the fear of the LORD,
And find the knowledge of God.

*Proverbs 2:4–5*

The fear of the LORD is the beginning of wisdom,
And the knowledge of the Holy One is understanding.

*Proverbs 9:10*

All the days of the afflicted are evil,
But he who is of a merry heart has a continual feast.
The fear of the LORD is the instruction of wisdom,
And before honor is humility.

*Proverbs 15:15, 33*


The fear of the LORD is the beginning of knowledge,
But fools despise wisdom and instruction.

*Proverbs 1:7*


The fear of the LORD leads to life,
And he who has it will abide in satisfaction;
He will not be visited with evil.

*Proverbs 19:23*


Then those who feared the LORD spoke to one another,
And the LORD listened and heard them;
So a book of remembrance was written before Him
For those who fear the LORD
And who meditate on His name.
"They shall be Mine," says the LORD of hosts,
"On the day that I make them My jewels.
And I will spare them
As a man spares his own son who serves him."

*Malachi 3:16—17*


In the fear of the LORD there is strong confidence,
And His children will have a place of refuge.

The fear of the LORD is a fountain of life,
To turn one away from the snares of death.

*Proverbs 14:26–27*

The fear of the LORD prolongs days,
But the years of the wicked will be shortened.

*Proverbs 10:27*

And to man He said,
"Behold, the fear of the Lord, that is wisdom,
And to depart from evil is understanding."

*Job 28:28*

Who is the man that fears the LORD?
Him shall He teach in the way He chooses.
He himself shall dwell in prosperity,
And his descendants shall inherit the earth.
The secret of the LORD is with those who fear Him,
And He will show them His covenant.

*Psalm 25:12–14*

For the LORD is great and greatly to be praised;
He is also to be feared above all gods.

*1 Chronicles 16:25*

In mercy and truth
Atonement is provided for iniquity;
And by the fear of the LORD one departs from evil.

*Proverbs 16:6*

The fear of the LORD is clean, enduring forever;
The judgments of the LORD are true and righteous altogether.

*Psalm 19:9*

Let us hear the conclusion of the whole matter:
Fear God and keep His commandments,
For this is man's all.
For God will bring every work into judgment,
Including every secret thing,
Whether good or evil.

*Ecclesiastes 12:13–14*

# WHAT IS THE SOVEREIGNTY OF GOD?

Great is the LORD, and greatly to be praised;
And His greatness is unsearchable.
One generation shall praise Your works to another,
And shall declare Your mighty acts.
Your kingdom is an everlasting kingdom,
And Your dominion endures throughout all generations.

*Psalm 145:3–4, 13*

All nations before Him are as nothing,
And they are counted by Him less than nothing and worthless.
To whom then will you liken God?
Or what likeness will you compare to Him?
"To whom then will you liken Me,
Or to whom shall I be equal?" says the Holy One.
Lift up your eyes on high,
And see who has created these things,
Who brings out their host by number;
He calls them all by name,
By the greatness of His might
And the strength of His power;
Not one is missing.
Have you not known?
Have you not heard?

The everlasting God, the LORD,
The Creator of the ends of the earth,
Neither faints nor is weary.
His understanding is unsearchable.

*Isaiah 40:17–18, 25–26, 28*

Thus says the LORD:
"Heaven is My throne,
And earth is My footstool.
Where is the house that you will build Me?
And where is the place of My rest?
For all those things My hand has made,
And all those things exist,"
says the LORD.
"But on this one will I look:
On him who is poor and of a contrite spirit,
And who trembles at My word."

*Isaiah 66:1–2*

For the LORD is our Judge,
The LORD is our Lawgiver,
The LORD is our King;
He will save us.

*Isaiah 33:22*

Then Moses said to God, "Indeed, when I come to the children of Israel and say to them, 'The God of your fathers has sent me to you,' and they say to me, 'What is His name?' what shall I say to them?"

And God said to Moses, "I AM WHO I AM." And He said, "Thus you shall say to the children of Israel, 'I AM has sent me to you.'"

*Exodus 3:13–14*

For with God nothing will be impossible.

*Luke 1:37*

Lord, You have been our dwelling place in all generations.
Before the mountains were brought forth,
Or ever You had formed the earth and the world,
Even from everlasting to everlasting, You are God.
You turn man to destruction,
And say, "Return, O children of men."
For a thousand years in Your sight
Are like yesterday when it is past,
And like a watch in the night.

*Psalm 90:1–4*

Now see that I, even I, am He,
And there is no God besides Me;
I kill and I make alive;
I wound and I heal;
Nor is there any who can deliver from My hand.
For I raise My hand to heaven,
And say, "As I live forever."

*Deuteronomy 32:39–40*

Where were you when I laid the foundations of the earth?

Tell Me, if you have understanding.
Who determined its measurements?
Surely you know!
Or who stretched the line upon it?
To what were its foundations fastened?
Or who laid its cornerstone,
When the morning stars sang together,
And all the sons of God shouted for joy?

*Job 38:4–7*

Whom have I in heaven but You?
And there is none upon earth that I desire besides You.

*Psalm 73:25*

This is the purpose that is purposed against the whole earth,
And this is the hand that is stretched out over all the nations.
For the LORD of hosts has purposed,
And who will annul it?
His hand is stretched out,
And who will turn it back?

*Isaiah 14:26–27*

For thus says the High and Lofty One
Who inhabits eternity, whose name is Holy:
"I dwell in the high and holy place,
With him who has a contrite and humble spirit,
To revive the spirit of the humble,
And to revive the heart of the contrite ones."

*Isaiah 57:15*

"Am I a God near at hand," says the LORD,
"And not a God afar off?
Can anyone hide himself in secret places,
So I shall not see him?" says the LORD;
"Do I not fill heaven and earth?" says the LORD.

*Jeremiah 23:23–24*


And when I saw Him, I fell at His feet as dead. But He laid His right hand on me, saying to me, "Do not be afraid; I am the First and the Last.

I am He who lives, and was dead, and behold, I am alive forevermore. Amen. And I have the keys of Hades and of Death."

*Revelation 1:17–18*


The heavens declare the glory of God;
And the firmament shows His handiwork.

*Psalm 19:1*


Behold, I am the LORD, the God of all flesh. Is there anything too hard for Me?

*Jeremiah 32:27*


In the beginning God created the heavens and the earth.
The earth was without form, and void; and darkness was on the face of the deep. And the Spirit of God was hovering over the face of the waters.
Then God said, "Let there be light"; and there was light.

*Genesis 1:1–3*

# How to Grasp Eternity

And I heard a loud voice from heaven saying, "Behold, the tabernacle of God is with men, and He will dwell with them, and they shall be His people. God Himself will be with them and be their God.

And God will wipe away every tear from their eyes; there shall be no more death, nor sorrow, nor crying. There shall be no more pain, for the former things have passed away."

Then He who sat on the throne said, "Behold, I make all things new." And He said to me, "Write, for these words are true and faithful."

And He said to me, "It is done! I am the Alpha and the Omega, the Beginning and the End. I will give of the fountain of the water of life freely to him who thirsts."

*Revelation 21:3–6*

But as it is written:
"Eye has not seen, nor ear heard,
Nor have entered into the heart of man
The things which God has prepared for those who love Him."

But God has revealed them to us through His Spirit. For the Spirit searches all things, yes, the deep things of God.

For what man knows the things of a man except the spirit

of the man which is in him? Even so no one knows the things of God except the Spirit of God.

> Violence shall no longer be heard in your land,
> Neither wasting nor destruction within your borders;
> But you shall call your walls Salvation,
> And your gates Praise.
> "The sun shall no longer be your light by day,
> Nor for brightness shall the moon give light to you;
> But the LORD will be to you an everlasting light,
> And your God your glory.
> Your sun shall no longer go down,
> Nor shall your moon withdraw itself;
> For the LORD will be your everlasting light,
> And the days of your mourning shall be ended."

*Isaiah 60:18–20*

The city had no need of the sun or of the moon to shine in it, for the glory of God illuminated it. The Lamb is its light.

And the nations of those who are saved shall walk in its light, and the kings of the earth bring their glory and honor into it.

Its gates shall not be shut at all by day (there shall be no night there).

And they shall bring the glory and the honor of the nations into it.

But there shall by no means enter it anything that defiles,

or causes an abomination or a lie, but only those who are written in the Lamb's Book of Life.

So when this corruptible has put on incorruption, and this mortal has put on immortality, then shall be brought to pass the saying that is written: "Death is swallowed up in victory."

"O Death, where is your sting?

O Hades, where is your victory?"

But thanks be to God, who gives us the victory through our Lord Jesus Christ.

*1 Corinthians 15:54—55, 57*

I was watching in the night visions,
And behold, One like the Son of man,
Coming with the clouds of heaven!
He came to the Ancient of Days,
And they brought Him near before Him.
Then to Him was given dominion and glory and a kingdom,
That all peoples, nations, and languages should serve Him.
His dominion is an everlasting dominion,
Which shall not pass away,
And His kingdom the one
Which shall not be destroyed.

*Daniel 7:13—14*

There are also celestial bodies and terrestrial bodies; but

the glory of the celestial is one, and the glory of the terrestrial is another.

So also is the resurrection of the dead. The body is sown in corruption, it is raised in incorruption.

It is sown in dishonor, it is raised in glory. It is sown in weakness, it is raised in power.

It is sown a natural body, it is raised a spiritual body. There is a natural body, and there is a spiritual body.

*1 Corinthians 15:40, 42–44*

Those who are wise shall shine
Like the brightness of the firmament,
And those who turn many to righteousness
Like the stars forever and ever.

*Daniel 12:3*

For now we see in a mirror, dimly, but then face to face. Now I know in part, but then I shall know just as I also am known.

*1 Corinthians 13:12*

Assuredly, I say to you, I will no longer drink of the fruit of the vine until that day when I drink it new in the kingdom of God.

*Mark 14:25*

He will swallow up death forever,
And the Lord God will wipe away tears from all faces;

The rebuke of His people
He will take away from all the earth;
For the LORD has spoken.

*Isaiah 25:8*

Surely goodness and mercy shall follow me
All the days of my life;
And I will dwell in the house of the LORD
Forever.

*Psalm 23:6*

# UNITING
## IN CHRIST

# WHAT IS THE FELLOWSHIP OF ALL BELIEVERS?

But now God has set the members, each one of them, in the body just as He pleased.

And if they were all one member, where would the body be?

But now indeed there are many members, yet one body.

And the eye cannot say to the hand, "I have no need of you"; nor again the head to the feet, "I have no need of you."

No, much rather, those members of the body which seem to be weaker are necessary.

And those members of the body which we think to be less honorable, on these we bestow greater honor; and our unpresentable parts have greater modesty,

but our presentable parts have no need. But God composed the body, having given greater honor to that part which lacks it,

that there should be no schism in the body, but that the members should have the same care for one another.

And if one member suffers, all the members suffer with it; or if one member is honored, all the members rejoice with it.

Now you are the body of Christ, and members individually.

*1 Corinthians 12:18—27*

Now, therefore, you are no longer strangers and foreigners, but fellow citizens with the saints and members of the household of God,

having been built on the foundation of the apostles and prophets, Jesus Christ Himself being the chief cornerstone,

in whom the whole building, being fitted together, grows into a holy temple in the Lord,

in whom you also are being built together for a dwelling place of God in the Spirit.

*Ephesians 2:19–22*


Finally, all of you be of one mind, having compassion for one another; love as brothers, be tenderhearted, be courteous;

not returning evil for evil or reviling for reviling, but on the contrary blessing, knowing that you were called to this, that you may inherit a blessing.

*1 Peter 3:8–9*


"For where two or three are gathered together in My name, I am there in the midst of them."

Then Peter came to Him and said, "Lord, how often shall my brother sin against me, and I forgive him? Up to seven times?"

Jesus said to him, "I do not say to you, up to seven times, but up to seventy times seven."

*Matthew 18:20–22*

He who says he is in the light, and hates his brother, is in darkness until now.

He who loves his brother abides in the light, and there is no cause for stumbling in him.

But he who hates his brother is in darkness and walks in darkness, and does not know where he is going, because the darkness has blinded his eyes.

*1 John 2:9–11*

God is faithful, by whom you were called into the fellowship of His Son, Jesus Christ our Lord.

Now I plead with you, brethren, by the name of our Lord Jesus Christ, that you all speak the same thing, and that there be no divisions among you, but that you be perfectly joined together in the same mind and in the same judgment.

*1 Corinthians 1:9–10*

For you are still carnal. For where there are envy, strife, and divisions among you, are you not carnal and behaving like mere men?

For when one says, "I am of Paul," and another, "I am of Apollos," are you not carnal?

Who then is Paul, and who is Apollos, but ministers through whom you believed, as the Lord gave to each one?

I planted, Apollos watered, but God gave the increase.

So then neither he who plants is anything, nor he who waters, but God who gives the increase.

Now he who plants and he who waters are one, and each one will receive his own reward according to his own labor.

For we are God's fellow workers; you are God's field, you are God's building.

*1 Corinthians 3:3–9*


You call Me Teacher and Lord, and you say well, for so I am.

If I then, your Lord and Teacher, have washed your feet, you also ought to wash one another's feet.

For I have given you an example, that you should do as I have done to you.

Most assuredly, I say to you, a servant is not greater than his master; nor is he who is sent greater than he who sent him.

If you know these things, blessed are you if you do them.

*John 13:13–17*


I do not pray for these alone, but also for those who will believe in Me through their word;

that they all may be one, as You, Father, are in Me, and I in You; that they also may be one in Us, that the world may believe that You sent Me.

And the glory which You gave Me I have given them, that they may be one just as We are one:

I in them, and You in Me; that they may be made perfect in one, and that the world may know that You have sent Me, and have loved them as You have loved Me.

*John 17:20–23*

Now John answered Him, saying, "Teacher, we saw someone who does not follow us casting out demons in Your name, and we forbade him because he does not follow us."

But Jesus said, "Do not forbid him, for no one who works a miracle in My name can soon afterward speak evil of Me.

For he who is not against us is on our side.

For whoever gives you a cup of water to drink in My name, because you belong to Christ, assuredly, I say to you, he will by no means lose his reward.

But whoever causes one of these little ones who believe in Me to stumble, it would be better for him if a millstone were hung around his neck, and he were thrown into the sea."

*Mark 9:38–42*


You also, as living stones, are being built up a spiritual house, a holy priesthood, to offer up spiritual sacrifices acceptable to God through Jesus Christ.

But you are a chosen generation, a royal priesthood, a holy nation, His own special people, that you may proclaim the praises of Him who called you out of darkness into His marvelous light.

*1 Peter 2:5, 9*


But God, who is rich in mercy, because of His great love with which He loved us,

even when we were dead in trespasses, made us alive together with Christ (by grace you have been saved), and raised us up together, and made us sit together in the heavenly places in Christ Jesus.

*Ephesians 2:4–6*

If we say that we have fellowship with Him, and walk in darkness, we lie and do not practice the truth.

But if we walk in the light as He is in the light, we have fellowship with one another, and the blood of Jesus Christ His Son cleanses us from all sin.

*1 John 1:6–7*

Behold, how good and how pleasant it is
For brethren to dwell together in unity!
It is like the precious oil upon the head,
Running down on the beard,
The beard of Aaron,
Running down on the edge of his garments.
It is like the dew of Hermon,
Descending upon the mountains of Zion;
For there the LORD commanded the blessing—
Life forevermore.

*Psalm 133:1–3*

He who is not with me is against Me, and he who does not gather with Me scatters abroad.

*Matthew 12:30*

And He stretched out His hand toward His disciples and said, "Here are My mother and My brothers!

For whoever does the will of My Father in heaven is My brother and sister and mother."

*Matthew 12:49–50*

Or do you not know that your body is the temple of the Holy Spirit who is in you, whom you have from God, and you are not your own?

For you were bought at a price; therefore glorify God in your body and in your spirit, which are God's.

*1 Corinthians 6:19–20*

There is neither Jew nor Greek, there is neither slave nor free, there is neither male nor female; for you are all one in Christ Jesus.

And if you are Christ's, then you are Abraham's seed, and heirs according to the promise.

*Galatians 3:28–29*

But you shall receive power when the Holy Spirit has come upon you; and you shall be witnesses to Me in Jerusalem, and in all Judea and Samaria, and to the end of the earth.

*Acts 1:8*

# What Is the Hope for Revival?

The Lord is not slack concerning His promise, as some count slackness, but is longsuffering toward us, not willing that any should perish but that all should come to repentance.

*2 Peter 3:9*

Arise, shine;
For your light has come!
And the glory of the LORD is risen upon you.
For behold, the darkness shall cover the earth,
And deep darkness the people;
But the LORD will arise over you,
And His glory will be seen upon you.

*Isaiah 60:1–2*

And they shall rebuild the old ruins,
They shall raise up the former desolations,
And they shall repair the ruined cities,
The desolations of many generations.
For as the earth brings forth its bud,
As the garden causes the things that are sown in it to spring
forth,

So the Lord God will cause righteousness and praise to spring forth before all the nations.

*Isaiah 61:4, 11*


The voice of one crying in the wilderness:
"Prepare the way of the LORD;
Make straight in the desert
A highway for our God.
Every valley shall be exalted
And every mountain and hill brought low;
The crooked places shall be made straight
And the rough places smooth;
The glory of the LORD shall be revealed,
And all flesh shall see it together;
For the mouth of the LORD has spoken."

*Isaiah 40:3–5*


All the ends of the world
Shall remember and turn to the LORD,
And all the families of the nations
Shall worship before You.
For the kingdom is the LORD's,
And He rules over the nations.

*Psalm 22:27–28*


Therefore be patient, brethren, until the coming of the Lord. See how the farmer waits for the precious fruit of the earth, waiting patiently for it until it receives the early and latter rain.

*James 5:7*

And it shall come to pass afterward
That I will pour out My Spirit on all flesh;
Your sons and your daughters shall prophesy,
Your old men shall dream dreams,
Your young men shall see visions.
And also on My menservants and on My maidservants
I will pour out My Spirit in those days.
And I will show wonders in the heavens and in the earth:
Blood and fire and pillars of smoke.
The sun shall be turned into darkness,
And the moon into blood,
Before the coming of the great and awesome day of the LORD.
And it shall come to pass
That whoever calls on the name of the LORD
Shall be saved.
For in Mount Zion and in Jerusalem there shall be
deliverance,
As the LORD has said,
Among the remnant whom the LORD calls.

*Joel 2:28–32*


And the Spirit and the bride say, "Come!" And let him who
hears say, "Come!" And let him who thirsts come. Whoever
desires, let him take the water of life freely.

*Revelation 22:17*

For the earth will be filled
With the knowledge of the glory of the LORD,
As the waters cover the sea.

*Habakkuk 2:14*

The LORD has made bare His holy arm
In the eyes of all the nations;
And all the ends of the earth shall see
The salvation of our God.
So shall He sprinkle many nations.
Kings shall shut their mouths at Him;
For what had not been told them they shall see,
And what they had not heard they shall consider.

*Isaiah 52:10, 15*

And this gospel of the kingdom will be preached in all the world as a witness to all the nations, and then the end will come.

*Matthew 24:14*

For the vision is yet for an appointed time;
But at the end it will speak, and it will not lie.
Though it tarries, wait for it;
Because it will surely come,
It will not tarry.

*Habakkuk 2:3*

There is no speech nor language
Where their voice is not heard.
Their line has gone out through all the earth,
And their words to the end of the world.
In them He has set a tabernacle for the sun,
Which is like a bridegroom coming out of his chamber,
And rejoices like a strong man to run its race.

*Psalm 19:3–5*


Behold, I will do a new thing,
Now it shall spring forth;
Shall you not know it?
I will even make a road in the wilderness
And rivers in the desert.

*Isaiah 43:19*


"The glory of this latter temple shall be greater than the former," says the LORD of hosts. "And in this place I will give peace," says the LORD of hosts.

*Haggai 2:9*


I will seek what was lost and bring back what was driven away, bind up the broken and strengthen what was sick; but I will destroy the fat and the strong, and feed them in judgment.

*Ezekiel 34:16*


Indeed the LORD has proclaimed
To the end of the world:

"Say to the daughter of Zion,
'Surely your salvation is coming;
Behold, His reward is with Him,
And His work before Him.'"
And they shall call them the Holy People,
The Redeemed of the LORD;
And you shall be called Sought Out,
A City Not Forsaken.

*Isaiah 62:11–12*

# WHAT ARE SIGNS OF THE END?

And Jesus answered and said to them: "Take heed that no one deceives you.

For many will come in My name, saying, 'I am the Christ,' and will deceive many.

And you will hear of wars and rumors of wars. See that you are not troubled; for all these things must come to pass, but the end is not yet.

For nation will rise against nation, and kingdom against kingdom. And there will be famines, pestilences, and earthquakes in various places.

All these are the beginning of sorrows.

Then they will deliver you up to tribulation and kill you, and you will be hated by all nations for My name's sake.

And then many will be offended, will betray one another, and will hate one another.

Then many false prophets will rise up and deceive many.

And because lawlessness will abound, the love of many will grow cold.

But he who endures to the end shall be saved.

And this gospel of the kingdom will be preached in all the world as a witness to all the nations, and then the end will come."

*Matthew 24:4—14*

Then two men will be in the field: one will be taken and the other left.

Watch therefore, for you do not know what hour your Lord is coming.

Therefore you also be ready, for the Son of Man is coming at an hour you do not expect.

*Matthew 24:40, 42, 44*

But know this, that in the last days perilous times will come:

For men will be lovers of themselves, lovers of money, boasters, proud, blasphemers, disobedient to parents, unthankful, unholy,

unloving, unforgiving, slanderers, without self-control, brutal, despisers of good,

traitors, headstrong, haughty, lovers of pleasure rather than lovers of God,

having a form of godliness but denying its power. And from such people turn away!

*2 Timothy 3:1–5*

Now the Spirit expressly says that in latter times some will depart from the faith, giving heed to deceiving spirits and doctrines of demons,

speaking lies in hypocrisy, having their own conscience seared with a hot iron,

forbidding to marry, and commanding to abstain from foods which God created to be received with thanksgiving by those who believe and know the truth.

*1 Timothy 4:1–3*

For the time will come when they will not endure sound doctrine, but according to their own desires, because they have itching ears, they will heap up for themselves teachers; and they will turn their ears away from the truth, and be turned aside to fables.

*2 Timothy 4:3–4*

And it shall come to pass in the last days, says God,
That I will pour out of My Spirit on all flesh;
Your sons and your daughters shall prophesy,
Your young men shall see visions,
Your old men shall dream dreams.
And on My menservants and on My maidservants
I will pour out My Spirit in those days;
And they shall prophesy.
I will show wonders in heaven above
And signs in the earth beneath:
Blood and fire and vapor of smoke.
The sun shall be turned into darkness,
And the moon into blood,
Before the coming of the great and awesome day of the Lord.
And it shall come to pass
That whoever calls on the name of the Lord
Shall be saved.

*Acts 2:17–21*

Indeed the Lord has proclaimed
To the end of the world:

"Say to the daughter of Zion,
'Surely your salvation is coming;
Behold, His reward is with Him,
And His work before Him.'"
And they shall call them The Holy People,
The Redeemed of the LORD;
And you shall be called Sought Out,
A City Not Forsaken.

*Isaiah 62:11–12*

So Christ was offered once to bear the sins of many. To those who eagerly wait for Him He will appear a second time, apart from sin, for salvation.

*Hebrews 9:28*

The earth shall reel to and fro like a drunkard,
And shall totter like a hut;
Its transgression shall be heavy upon it,
And it will fall, and not rise again.
It shall come to pass in that day
That the LORD will punish on high the host of exalted ones,
And on the earth the kings of the earth.
They will be gathered together,
As prisoners are gathered in the pit,
And will be shut up in the prison;
After many days they will be punished.

*Isaiah 24:20–22*

Knowing this first: that scoffers will come in the last days, walking according to their own lusts,

and saying, "Where is the promise of His coming? For since the fathers fell asleep, all things continue as they were from the beginning of creation."

But, beloved, do not forget this one thing, that with the Lord one day is as a thousand years, and a thousand years as one day.

The Lord is not slack concerning His promise, as some count slackness, but is longsuffering toward us, not willing that any should perish but that all should come to repentance.

But the day of the Lord will come as a thief in the night, in which the heavens will pass away with a great noise, and the elements will melt with fervent heat; both the earth and the works that are in it will be burned up.

*2 Peter 3:3–4, 8–10*

But you, beloved, remember the words which were spoken before by the apostles of our Lord Jesus Christ:

how they told you that there would be mockers in the last time who would walk according to their own ungodly lusts.

These are sensual persons, who cause divisions, not having the Spirit.

But you, beloved, building yourselves up on your most holy faith, praying in the Holy Spirit,

keep yourselves in the love of God, looking for the mercy of our Lord Jesus Christ unto eternal life.

*Jude 17–21*

Likewise also the men, leaving the natural use of the woman, burned in their lust for one another, men with men committing what is shameful, and receiving in themselves the penalty of their error which was due.

*Romans 1:27*

And in the latter time of their kingdom,
When the transgressors have reached their fullness,
A king shall arise,
Having fierce features,
Who understands sinister schemes.

*Daniel 8:23*

He causes all, both small and great, rich and poor, free and slave, to receive a mark on their right hand or on their foreheads,

and that no one may buy or sell except one who has the mark or the name of the beast, or the number of his name.

Here is wisdom. Let him who has understanding calculate the number of the beast, for it is the number of a man: His number is 666.

*Revelation 13:16–18*

Heaven and earth shall pass away, but My words will by no means pass away...

*Matthew 24:35*

# MY PRAYER LIST

# MY PRAYER LIST

## MY PRAYER LIST

# MY PRAYER LIST

# MY PRAYER LIST

# MY PRAYER LIST

# PERSONAL STUDY NOTES

# PERSONAL STUDY NOTES

# PERSONAL STUDY NOTES

# PERSONAL STUDY NOTES

# PERSONAL STUDY NOTES

# PERSONAL STUDY NOTES